CONTAINER GARDENING

CONTAINER GARDENING

FLOWERS AND FOLIAGE
IN POTS, TUBS AND BASKETS

THE
APPLE
PRESS

Picture Credits

A QUINTET BOOK

Published by The Apple Press
6 Blundell Street
London N7 9BH

Reprinted 1992

ISBN 1-85076-278-3

This book was designed and produced by
Quintet Publishing Limited
6 Blundell Street
London N7 9BH

Creative Director: Peter Bridgewater
Art Director: Ian Hunt
Designer: Madeline Serre
Project Editor: Caroline Beattie
Editor: Carol Hupping
Picture Researcher: Liz Eddison

Typeset in Great Britain by
Central Southern Typesetters, Eastbourne
Manufactured in Hong Kong by
Regent Publishing Services Limited
Printed in Hong Kong by
Leefung-Asco Printers Limited

David Bradfield: back jacket, pages 20 (top) and
46.

Samuel Dobie & Son Ltd: page 88/b.

Liz Eddison: pages 6, 10/tr & bl, 12/tr, 14/t, 16, 19,
20/b, 21/l, 24/t, 25, 26/b, 30, 32, 34/b, 37/tr, 39, 41/r,
44, 48/b, 52, 58, 60, 61, 63, 64, 86 and 93.

Harry Smith Horticultural Photographic
Collection: pages 7, 11/r, 12/l, 14/b, 17, 18, 22/bl,
23/b, 24/b, 26/t, 28/b, 34/t, 35, 40, 41/l, 42/tr, 57/b,
68, 69/tr, 72, 73/b, 74, 78/r, 84/t and 92.

Bill Heritage: pages 70, 73/tr.

Peter McHoy: pages 10/tl, 12/br, 13/t, 15, 22/tr, 23/t,
29, 31/t, 33, 38, 43, 45, 48/t, 54, 73/tl, 79, 80, 82, 83,
84/b and 85.

R A Meredith & Son Ltd: page 21/r.

Photos Horticultural (Michael and Lois Warren):
front jacket, pages 2, 8, 13/b, 27, 36, 37/bl, 50, 53,
56, 69/b, 76, 78/l, 81 and 88/t.

Photo/Nats: © Liz Ball: pages 31/b and 42/bl.
© Gay Bumgarner: pages 10/br, 11/l and 66.
© Priscilla Connell: page 28/t.
© J A Lynch: page 67/t.
© Robert E Lyons: page 51.
© David M Stone: page 55.
© Marilyn Wood: page 62.

Rob Shone: artwork on pages 49, 50, 59, 72, 89, 90,
91

Contents

Introduction

Container gardening, despite being so very fashionable today, is almost as old as gardening itself. Plants have been grown in receptacles of all kinds by almost every culture for centuries, including the ancient civilizations of China, Egypt, Greece and Rome.

One of the reasons it is so popular now is because it fits in so well with the trend towards small gardens. Containers make gardening space where little or none is otherwise available.

But container gardening is not all to do with making the most out of limited space. Design-conscious people realize that, if chosen carefully, ornamental containers can very much help in garden design by creating mood or 'atmosphere'.

There is a wide range of containers available today, including traditional flower pots, both plain and ornamental. There are tubs in all shapes, sizes and designs, and these are probably among the most useful for the container gardener. Traditional wooden tubs and barrels, vases and narrow-necked urns in classical styles, shallow bowls, and long troughs are all suitable. And window boxes, wall pots and hanging baskets are good for filling vertical space. Then there are novelty containers such as old chimney pots and wooden wheelbarrows. The most revolutionary container to appear in recent years is the growing bag, primarily designed for vegetable culture. What you use as containers for growing plants is limited almost only by your imagination.

Containers should be chosen with care to ensure they match the surroundings and fit in gracefully with the overall garden design. For instance, traditional or classical

LEFT *Almost anything can be used as a plant container. An old metal bucket is filled with pelargoniums and ivy, two favourites for containers. The container would have to be wintered in a frost-free greenhouse.*

styles may look out of place in a contemporary setting and, conversely, the clean, uncluttered lines of many modern containers would not fit easily into a period garden.

Containers can be used for growing plants in various parts of the garden. The most obvious place is the patio, but any other hard area could be suitable, too. Walls of the house, garage and other outbuildings can be adorned with window boxes, hanging baskets and the like, while lightweight containers of all kinds provide the ideal means of growing plants on balconies and roof gardens.

In many climates it is possible to obtain colour and interest all year round with carefully planned plantings.

The range of plants that can be grown in containers is wide, from small trees, through climbers, to shrubs, hardy perennials, bedding plants and even aquatics. Many fruits and vegetables, too, can be grown in large pots, tubs and barrels.

Container gardening has many attributes. It is ideal where space is very limited and can turn a patio, balcony, sunny porch, drive or rooftop into a vibrant, colourful growing space. Even if growing room is not an issue, a container can make it possible to grow plants not suited to the existing garden soil, for instance, making space for acid-loving rhododendrons that will not thrive in limy soils. Practical matters aside, beautiful plants flourishing in attractive containers add character and style to any outdoor area.

Of course, container gardening is not without its problems: frequent watering is a must in warm weather and regular feeding is necessary in spring and summer. Potting soil should be replaced regularly, and container plants are more susceptible to freezing during very cold weather. But for most people the pleasure that is to be gained from growing plants in containers far outweighs the problems.

ABOVE *A classic combination – zonal pelargoniums (geraniums), petunias and trailing blue lobelia – in an equally classic painted wooden tub.*

1

Containers for Patios

Visit almost any garden centre and you will find a large range of ornamental containers suitable for use on patios. They come in many styles, shapes and sizes.

Unless you want a somewhat bizarre effect, it is generally sensible to choose modern styles for contemporary houses and gardens, and traditional styles for period settings. The containers should appear to be part of the overall garden design and not as though added as an afterthought.

Container size is important, particularly its depth, to allow sufficient room for soil and plant roots and enough moss so that the soil does not dry out rapidly in warm weather. As a guide, a realistic minimum size for a patio tub is 30cm (12in) in both diameter and depth. In a container of this size you will be able to plant several bedding plants or a single small shrub. However, more effective bedding-plant designs can be created in tubs with both a diameter and a depth of 45–60cm (18–24in). Something in this range would hold a larger shrub, conifer, climber or small tree.

CONTAINERS FOR MODERN SETTINGS

Generally containers in contemporary styles have clean simple lines, and these are ideally suited to modern settings.

Many are formed of concrete, a material which can look most attractive if moulded well and imaginatively by the manufacturer. As with many products, there are both good and bad examples.

Other containers are formed of reconstituted stone, a mix of finely crushed stone and cement. The manufacturers form this into a doughlike consistency and press it into moulds. The result is a container which looks almost as if it has been formed from solid stone.

Plastic containers are also available, mainly in tubs and troughs; these look what they are – comparatively inexpensive. However, from a practical point of view most do a good job, but are perhaps best hidden as much as possible with trailing plants.

Tubs in concrete or reconstituted stone are probably the most useful containers for growing plants on a patio. The rectangular shape of troughs, made from similar materials, provides relief from the usual round containers and allows for some different plant arrangements.

Back in the 1950s a concrete container of revolutionary design appeared on the

OPPOSITE *Large terracotta flower-pots are very popular containers for both modern and period settings. These contain pink lilies impatiens and white hydrangeas, a subtle but charming colour design. The impatiens need replacing annually.*

LEFT AND BELOW *Troughs offer an alternative shape and are obtainable in various materials, including terracotta, plastic and* concrete. *This enables you to match containers with the design of your house and garden.*

ABOVE *A modern patio calls for containers in contemporary styles. Many, such as these large tubs, are made from concrete, and can, if desired, be hidden with trailing plants. Others such as the large wooden containers* ABOVE RIGHT *are attractive in their own right and allow for some ambitious planting designs.*

market. This was the shallow bowl, which looked superb with the architecture of the time. This type of container is still available and still looks good with today's architecture. The problem with it is lack of depth. The shallow soil dries out quickly in warm weather, so frequent watering is needed. These bowls are best planted with summer bedding plants such as pelargoniums, petunias and scarlet salvias, and with spring bedding like tulips and forget-me-nots. The brighter the colours, the better.

Concrete or reconstituted-stone containers are generally pale in colour, so if you want more colour from the containers themselves opt for terracotta clay. This is the traditional material for making pots and the like and is a lovely warm orange colour. You can buy ordinary plain (undecorated) flower pots in terracotta, and they come in a wide range of sizes, including diameters of 30, 45 and 60cm (12, 18 and 24in) and larger.

Be sure to buy frost-proof pots; these do

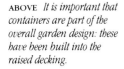

ABOVE *It is important that containers are part of the overall garden design: these have been built into the raised decking.*

ABOVE RIGHT *Large simple concrete containers are ideally suited to modern patios and allow for adventurous permanent planting designs which can be set off with large pebbles.*

not flake or crack during extreme weather conditions.

You can also buy plastic pots in terracotta colour, but these are more suitable for utility purposes than for ornamental use, and most people much prefer the real thing on the patio. Also, they are very light in weight and liable to be blown over if planted with a tall shrub or tree, especially if a light peat-based potting soil is used.

CHOOSING FOR PERIOD SETTINGS

Readily available are terracotta clay pots. Some are very ornate classical styles, dec-

orated with swags, fruits and the like. These look superb in period settings and, surprisingly, do not look out of place in more modern gardens. For a striking summer display plant them with red pelargoniums and violet heliotrope.

Classical-style, often highly ornate imitation-stone urns, vases and jars are an excellent choice for period settings. Keep in mind, though, that urns have very narrow necks which make them difficult to plant. Indeed, you cannot really create planting designs in them. A specimen plant might be suitable, such as a New Zealand cabbage palm, with its fountain of grassy foliage. Or a trailing plant might be good, such as a variegated ivy.

Vases and jars generally have wider openings and therefore lend themselves to more adventurous planting.

Large, square wooden tubs, after the style of those used in the gardens of Versailles in France, are excellent for displays of bedding, and there is no better container in which to grow small trees and large shrubs or conifers. Traditionally they are used for orange trees, and they are moved under cover in the winter for protection against frost. These tubs, supported on short legs, are generally painted white, although you might prefer to paint them to match the house if you want a coordinated effect.

There are also other sorts of containers suitable for patios in period settings. For instance, you might come across old stone troughs, or perhaps lead cisterns. Things like these might come into the realms of collectors' items – antiques which command a very high price. But if you want to spend the money it is worth bearing in mind that such items steadily increase in value over the years and can prove to be a good investment.

These containers are usually very deep so they can be densely planted. Sometimes it is possible to buy replicas of old stone troughs or cisterns which, of course, are much more affordable.

ABOVE *Period settings call for containers in classical styles, such as this reconstituted-stone trough.*

LEFT *Bushy plants, such as shrubby cinquefoils (potentilla) create a balanced design when planted in a tall, upright container on a pedestal.*

Containers are very good for creating focal points in garden design. **OPPOSITE TOP LEFT** *Tuberous begonias in a warm terracotta bowl in a classical style.* **OPPOSITE BOTTOM LEFT** *Stone containers come in many styles and sizes. This cistern-like one is planted with pink verbena and grey Helichrysum petiolatum.* **OPPOSITE TOP RIGHT** *Pedestal-mounted bowls help to create height on a patio and come in traditional and modern styles.* **OPPOSITE BOTTOM RIGHT** *This attractively-weathered terracotta jar has the advantage of depth but the disadvantage of a small-diameter top.*

CONTAINERS FOR THE COUNTRY GARDEN PATIO

In an informal or natural setting wood is usually most appropriate, so for a country garden patio consider wooden tubs or half barrels, or if the area is quite large, perhaps even full-size barrels. All are spacious and deep and so are ideal for permanent plants like shrubs, small trees and roses. Very often they are left in their natural colour, simply treated occasionally with a clear *horticultural* wood preservative. When buying containers made from real barrels, make sure they have drainage holes in the base. If not, 2.5cm (1in) diameter holes are easily drilled. An average-size barrel should have about five holes in the base.

Although more difficult to find, wooden troughs, often supported on four short legs and specially made for plants, are a good choice for a country garden patio, too.

Old clay chimney pots are becoming very popular as patio containers. Demand exceeds supply, so some enterprizing man-

ABOVE *An imaginative use for an old fireplace: it has been set into a wall and contains colourful bedding plants.*

BELOW *Currently popular for country-garden patios are old chimney pots. This one contains houseleeks.*

BELOW *Half barrels look good in country gardens. This one contains annual helichrysum, an old-fashioned everlasting flower.*

ufacturers are producing imitations. These pots are exceptionally tall but unfortunately have only a small diameter, roughly 15–22cm (6–9in), so planting designs for individual pots are out of the question. However, a very pleasing arrangement can be made by grouping several chimney pots together and planting different specimens in each. For instance, for a summer garden, some pots could contain trailing plants like petunias or lobelia, and others taller, more bushy subjects such as zonal pelargoniums or impatiens (busy lizzie).

Novelty containers that can sometimes be seen in country gardens are old wooden wheelbarrows, overflowing with cascading summer bedding plants like petunias, ivy-leaf pelargoniums and trailing fuchsias. Actually a wheelbarrow is quite a practical container since it is deepened to hold a good amount of soil. When the plants have finished flowering it can simply be wheeled away to a spare part of the garden, planted with other specimens for the next season, and then wheeled back into position as the new plants are coming into flower.

ARRANGING CONTAINERS

One of the least imaginative ways of using containers on a patio is to dot them around singly and haphazardly. Containers are far better grouped together, perhaps in groups of three or five, depending on the space available. This allows you to create some pleasing and coordinated designs.

For instance, a container or two at the back of a group could be planted with permanent evergreen or deciduous shrubs.

BELOW *An old wash-stand has been filled with zonal pelargoniums (geraniums) and ivy, a novel idea for a tiny basement garden. The window-sill contains a collection of scented-leaved pelargoniums.*

In due season these would flower and be features in their own right. But they would also make excellent background for temporary plants, such as summer bedding plants, spring bedding plants or bulbs. In effect, you can plan groups as you would in a mixed garden border.

You may wish to plan for specific seasons. For instance, a group for autumn might include a Japanese maple in a back container for autumn leaf colour, while the containers in the front of the group might be planted with dwarf outdoor chrysanthemums and bedding dahlias. A grouping for mild winters might include as background the evergreen shrubs *Mahonia japonica,* with fragrant yellow flowers, and the white-flowered laurustinus; the front containers could be filled with winter-flowering pansies.

A spring group could have a deciduous magnolia as a background plant, such as

the white star magnolia with its white starry flowers; or *M. soulangiana,* with its large goblet-shaped, purple-flushed blooms. Spring-flowering bulbs would go well with these magnolias, particularly grape hyacinths and polyanthus in blue shades.

For summer, try one of the evergreen escallonias as a background subject. These have flowers in shades of pink or red and bloom for a long period. The foliage makes a good backdrop for colourful summer bedding plants in colours which match the flowers of the escallonias, like red or pink pelargoniums, salvias and impatiens.

Fruit trees grouped together are very decorative when in blossom and in fruit. A collection of dwarf evergreen conifers can also be attractive. Ideas are limited only by your imagination.

Sometimes a formal arrangement of containers is appropriate for a particular setting. For instance, twin slow-growing conifers

of columnar habit, such as Lawson cypress variety 'Ellwoodii', Irish juniper or Irish yew, could be placed on either side of a door in identical tubs, and through the years, carefully trimmed to the same shape. If the patio has a particular entrance, it could be flanked by twin conifers; so could steps which lead on to a patio. Here, place the tubs at the top of the steps. In a very formal situation identical plants are sometimes set in each of the four corners of the patio.

If conifers do not appeal to you for these situations, then consider formal clipped bushes of holly, box or sweet bay. You could even have topiary specimens of these, such as mop-headed bays or hollies, or spirals of box. Topiary specimens can now be bought ready formed – but they are expensive.

Fruit trees can also be used in a similar way. Citrus fruits, such as oranges, look particularly effective in a formal setting.

RIGHT *A popular idea today, especially with owners of modern houses, is to have designs in single colours, which are often coordinated with the house decor. This warm colour theme is provided by pelargoniums, petunias and fuchsias. Other possibilities include marigolds, dahlias and scarlet salvias.*

COLOUR FROM SEASONAL PLANTS

Bedding plants, annuals and bulbs that bloom in various seasons are among the most popular groups of plants for providing colour on the patio.

ARRANGING PLANTS

First, some general hints on arranging plants effectively in patio containers. With mixed plantings it is generally recommended that a tallish plant, or group of plants, be set in the centre of the container to ensure height in the design. Surround this with shorter plants. Then, if space permits, even shorter subjects, or preferably trailers, can be planted around the edge. This arrangement is far more interesting than a perfectly flat design that is the result of using plants all of the same height.

Containers which are placed against walls should be arranged so that the tall plant, or group of tall plants, is at the back of the

OPPOSITE *Patio containers can be arranged with a tall plant in the centre to create height (here a New Zealand cabbage palm has been used), surrounded by shorter plants (such as pelargoniums), silver-leaved cineraria plus trailing kinds around the edge (for example, lobelia). Other tall plants that can be used include Indian shot and castor oil plant.*

container and the shorter plants are in front.

COLOUR DESIGNS

Colour designs are very much the personal choice of the gardener. Some people like the traditional idea of mixed colours in their containers, while others will go for single colours, perhaps coordinating them with the house decor. For instance, pink designs are very popular and create a 'warm' atmosphere. Red is a difficult colour, as it can be overpowering if used to excess, but when carefully used as an accent colour it can be very striking. For a sunny look choose yellows, perhaps with some whites, or with accents of orange. 'Cooler' designs can be created with blue flowers, and green and white designs are extremely restful.

There are plenty of bedding plants in all of these colours. More and more single colours (as opposed to mixtures of colours) are becoming available among bedding plants, and this makes it easier to control colours and achieve well-coordinated designs.

SOILS AND PLANTING

Containers for bedding plants, annuals and bulbs can be filled with peat-based potting soil. Some gardeners prefer a soil which contains loam, peat and sand; this is also suitable, particularly for small evergreen shrubs that remain in their containers throughout the year. It is best to change the soil completely every two years, replacing it with a fresh batch that has not had its nutrients used up.

In mild climates spring bedding plants and spring-flowering bulbs are planted in mid-autumn, as soon as the summer or autumn display is over.

These are cleared out when they have completed their display in the spring. The plants are discarded as they start to deteriorate after the first season, even though some are perennial and may survive for a number of years. Bulbs can be temporarily

ABOVE *Today the traditional idea of mixed colours as provided by the antirrhinums is favoured more by owners of cottage or country gardens. Sweet alyssum, another favourite cottage-garden annual, is valued for its delicious honey scent.*

LEFT *A green kochia or burning bush has been used as a centrepiece for strongly coloured impatiens (busy lizzie) and contrasting foliage plants. The impatiens need regular dead-heading.*

ABOVE *A cool white and grey design for summer, using standard white daisy-flowered marguerites, with white petunias and grey-leaved* Helichrysum petiolatum *to balance the design.*

ABOVE RIGHT *When changing seasonal designs in the traditional way, it is important to avoid disturbing any permanent residents. However, the introduction of ready-planted plastic modules, which are simply placed together in patio containers, has made seasonal changes quick and easy.*

replanted in a spare piece of ground to complete their growth; if they are not allowed to grow until their leaves naturally wilt, they will not be strong enough to bloom the following year. Then they are lifted, dried off, and stored cool and dry under cover until planting time again.

Summer bedding plants and annuals are planted wherever there is room for them in late spring or early summer. All of those recommended here are frost tender and would be damaged or killed if planted out before the last frost in spring.

Small evergreen shrubs are best planted in midspring or early autumn; at these times

they establish quickly. Evergreens can be planted on their own in containers; or they can share containers with spring or summer bedding – a popular combination among container gardeners. In either case, they should be considered permanent residents, as most will suffer from transplanting.

Changing seasonal designs is now easy, thanks to the availability at garden centres of ready-planted plastic modules, each containing a number of well-developed plants. These plants, modules and all, are simply placed in patio containers to create instant displays. You can buy plants that are coming into flower so that there is not the long, boring period between planting and flowering that sometimes occurs with traditional planting and which is particularly applicable to spring bedding.

Plants and bulbs are generally set close together in containers for optimum effect. They need some room to develop, though, so leave a little space around each. Arrange the plants so that the foliage is not quite touching.

Unless otherwise stated, all plants and bulbs should be grown in sunny positions. If your sun is limited, you will be pleased to find some plants that will grow in shade in the pages that follow.

SPRING COLOUR

Spring colour can be created with traditional spring bedding and other plants, and with bulbs. Such plantings are recommended only for areas where the winters are not too severe (not below −12°C/10°F).

BEDDING AND OTHER PLANTS

Many of the traditional spring bedding plants do well in containers:

WALLFLOWERS *(Cheiranthus cheiri)* − These have lovely flowers in many colours of red, yellow, orange and pink shades. They are available in mixtures or as separate colours.

Also recommended is the Siberian wall-flower *(C. allionii)*, a smaller, bushier plant with orange or yellow by interplanting wall-flowers with dwarf or low-growing tulips.

FORGET-ME-NOTS *(Myosotis sylvatica)* − These delicate flowers create a beautiful blue haze through which tulips could grow. They tolerate shade.

POLYANTHUS *(Primula polyantha)* − Poly-anthus are low-growing, shade-tolerant plants with a very long flowering period. They come in shades of blue, yellow, pink, orange, lavender, red and white, in mixtures or separate colours. Try growing dwarf or low-growing tulips or hyacinths through them.

DOUBLE DAISIES *(Bellis perennis* varieties) − Available in shades of red, pink and also white, these make an excellent carpet for dwarf tulips or hyacinths.

PANSIES (*Viola* x *wittrockiana*) − These flower over an incredibly long period, and for spring colour in areas with mild winters, winter-flowering varieties planted the pre-vious autumn will still be in bloom in spring. Alternatively plant spring-flowering varie-

RIGHT *There are many small bulbs which provide spring colour in containers, such as large-flowered Dutch crocuses, seen here in a herb pot, which need a very sunny spot for the flowers to open. Other small bulbs that would look good planted like this include grape hyacinths, scillas and chionodoxas.*

BELOW *Dwarf or low-growing tulips are popular for spring, combining well with blue forget-me-nots. Both are planted in autumn and wintered outdoors. Other good companions for tulips are polyanthus, double daisies and Siberian wallflowers.*

ties. Again mixtures or separate colours are available. Pansies look good on their own, but would be enhanced with ivies cascading over the edge of the container. An evergreen shrub such as a *Euonymus fortunei* could form a centrepiece. Pansies and the euonymus will be happy in partial shade.

AUBRIETA – For something rather different try mass planting aubrieta in containers for spring colour. These trailing plants produce masses of flowers in shades of purple, blue, red or pink. They are actually best known as perennial rock-garden plants, but after flowering they could be lifted and planted elsewhere in the garden. A dwarf conifer such as Lawson cypress variety 'Ellwoodii' would make a good centrepiece, or one of the more spreading types such as a *Juniperus* x *media* variety.

DRUMSTICK PRIMROSE *(Primula denticulata)* – Really a woodland plant, this primrose nevertheless looks marvellous mass-planted in tubs in a position with partial shade, perhaps grouped with small evergreen shrubs. It likes steadily moist soil. After it has produced its globe-shaped mauve, purple, red or white flowers, lift

the plants and replant elsewhere in the garden.

BULBS

Dwarf or low-growing tulips are popular for containers, and among the most widely planted are the varieties of *Tulipa greigii* and *T. kaufmanniana,* the former having purple-marked foliage. Also recommended are the short double early and single early varieties. All of these are available in separate colours if you want to produce coordinated designs. For instance, you may want to try yellow tulips with yellow polyanthus.

Hyacinths *(Hyacinthus)* are high on the list of popular container bulbs. They not only provide scent but come in a wide range of separate colours.

There are many dwarf and miniature bulbs suitable for containers, such as squills *(Scilla)*, glory of the snow *(Chionodoxa)*, grape hyacinths *(Muscari)* and daffodils *(Narcissus)*, all of which look lovely planted around small evergreen shrubs with ivies cascading over the edge. If you have sufficient containers and have winters which are not too severe (not below −12°C/10°F) these small bulbs could be left undisturbed for several years. If not, lift them after flowering, as described earlier.

LEFT *A superb combination for spring: a white star magnolia surrounded by cream-coloured pansies; the latter need to be planted shallowly as the magnolia is a permanent resident. Another pleasing combination is forsythia and small spring bulbs.*

BELOW *A traditional design with spring-flowering bulbs: golden daffodils and dwarf scarlet tulips. Both need dead-heading and can be lifted and gradually dried off after flowering to make way for summer bedding plants.*

SUMMER COLOUR

There are many summer bedding plants and annuals that can provide beautiful vivid colour in patio containers. They may be grown alone or several different types of plants can be grouped together, ideally with a tallish plant in the centre of the container to give height.

TO CREATE HEIGHT

There are several tall plants that are frequently used to give height:

NEW ZEALAND CABBAGE PALM *(Cordyline australis)* – This perennial has a fountain of narrow, grassy foliage. It can be kept from year to year, if protected from frost.

INDIAN SHOT *(Canna* x *generalis)* – This tender perennial can be kept from year to year if overwintered in a dormant state in frost-free conditions. Large dramatic foliage, either plain green or purple, and spikes of large, colourful, lily-like flowers are features of this plant.

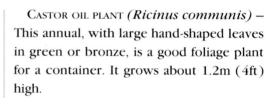

ABOVE Helichrysum petiolatum, *a popular foliage 'mixer' for summer bedding plants like trailing verbena.*

BELOW *Permanent foliage plants, including spectacular New Zealand cabbage palms, make good backgrounds for colourful summer bedding. Yuccas are another good example.*

CASTOR OIL PLANT *(Ricinus communis)* – This annual, with large hand-shaped leaves in green or bronze, is a good foliage plant for a container. It grows about 1.2m (4ft) high.

JOSEPH'S COAT *(Amaranthus tricolor)* – This annual is another foliage plant good for creating height. It grows to about 60–90cm (2–3ft) high and has large, oval, basically red leaves.

Other foliage plants that are often mixed with summer bedders to create contrast in colour and texture include:

Helichrysum petiolatum – This is a trailing or spreading tender perennial with small rounded grey leaves.

SILVER-LEAVED CINERARIA OR DUSTY MILLER *(Senecio cineraria, Cineraria maritima)* – This perennial with grey-lobed and deeply cut leaves is usually treated as an annual and discarded at the end of the season. These two are especially suitable for combining with plants that have strongly coloured flowers, such as scarlet or brilliant red pelargoniums or salvias.

TOP BEDDING PLANTS AND ANNUALS

All of the plants described below are classed as temporary plants, because they are dis-

ABOVE *Tuberous begonias and geraniums are two of the most popular plants for summer colour in containers. Both live for several years if wintered in frost-free conditions.*

BELOW RIGHT *A small sunken pool has been edged with a container planted with a standard fuchsia which is complemented by the hot colours of the petunias.*

carded (because they start to deteriorate or may become too large) when the flower display is over in the autumn, even though many of them are perennial and therefore capable of living for a number of years. Annuals die naturally when they have finished flowering.

WAX BEGONIAS *(Begonia semperflorens)* – These are dwarf, bushy plants that produce a mass of flowers in shades of red, pink or white from early summer until the frosts of autumn. They are available in mixtures or separate colours and are ideally suited to single-colour designs: for instance, pink begonias with pink impatiens (busy lizzie) and pink ivy-leaved pelargoniums.

These begonias are suitable for growing in shade, as are the large-flowered double tuberous begonias that come in a wide range of bright and pastel colours. These look attractive mixed with celosias and coleus.

ZONAL PELARGONIUMS *(Pelargonium x hortorum)* – Popularly known as geraniums, these are important container plants relishing full sun and tolerating dry conditions. These days most are seed raised and come in a wide range of colours: shades of red, scarlet, orange, pink, purple and white. They are ideal for single-colour designs: try

red pelargoniums with red verbenas, petunias or celosias. You may prefer to mix silver-leaved cineraria or *Helichrysum petiolatum* with strong-coloured pelargoniums to help tone them down.

IVY-LEAVED PELARGONIUMS *(Pelargonium peltatum)* – These are perhaps more useful in elevated containers such as window boxes or hanging baskets, but they are useful, too, for trailing over the edges of patio containers. They really do have ivy-shaped leaves, and their flowers come in shades of pink or red, plus white.

FUCHSIAS – For containers, greenhouse bush varieties are recommended, but trailing greenhouse varieties are useful, too, for the edges of containers. They flower best in sun, but they will also perform well in partial shade. The bell-shaped flowers are produced in profusion all summer and come in various colour combinations such as blue and red or red and white. Various plants can be mixed effectively with fuchsias, such as blue heliotrope (this would

RIGHT *Impatiens or busy lizzie have become very popular for summer colour in recent years. Here they are effectively combined with red-and gold-leaved coleus. Other good companions are ivies and wax begonias.*

BELOW *With container gardening it is easy to create height in designs. Petunias come in many colours and are suitable for all kinds of containers. The hanging baskets contain ivy-leaved pelargoniums.*

make a good centrepiece), blue ageratum (could be used as an edging) and coleus, whose multicoloured foliage creates striking contrast.

IMPATIENS OR BUSY LIZZIE *(Impatiens wallerana)* – These bedding plants have shot to the top of the popularity charts in recent years. They are dwarf, compact plants that flower continuously from early summer until the autumn frosts arrive. The flowers are in all shades of red, pink and orange, plus white. They come in mixtures, but separate colours are available and are so useful for creating single-colour designs. A centrepiece of New Zealand cabbage palm is particularly effective with impatiens. Alternatively try a castor oil plant or Indian shot. All of these provide a striking contrast in shape and texture.

Impatiens are among the best summer bedding plants for growing in shade. The soil should be kept constantly moist as they dislike dry conditions.

DAHLIAS – Dwarf bedding dahlias flower from early or mid summer until the frosts arrive. The flowers are single or double and most strains come in mixtures of colours, but in recent years single colours such as yellow and red have been available. Yellow dahlias would be ideal for single-colour schemes, combining them with yellow bedding calceolarias or gazanias. Dahlias like plenty of water and should be grown in full sun.

SCARLET SALVIAS *(Salvia splendens)* – Due to their strong colour these can be difficult to use; nonetheless, they are popular bedding plants. When mass planted the effect can be rather overpowering. To tone down this 'hot' colour, use plenty of foliage such as silver-leaved cineraria. Dwarf evergreen shrubs can also act as a foil, and in a group of containers make sure salvias have a leafy shrub as a background. Lime-green nicotiana also makes a good companion for salvias.

PETUNIAS – These rank high on the list of popular summer bedding plants and are ideal for container work. Most have a bushy habit, but some are trailing, and these trailing ones are more suitable for elevated containers. The colour range is enormous and in both mixtures and separate colours. The flowers are trumpet-shaped or, in some varieties, double. The most satisfactory petunias for bedding are the multiflora varieties, with masses of small, rain-resistant flowers. Petunias are generally used as companions for other bedding plants rather than grown on their own. They combine particularly well with pelargoniums and fuchsias. Try blue or purple petunias with orange pelargoniums or, for a single-colour design, pink petunias and pink pelargoniums.

ABOVE This mixture of summer bedding plants and annuals would be ideal for an English cottage garden. It includes begonias, petunias, lobelia, calceolaria and mimulus. Bear in mind that all plants must require the same conditions for such a design to succeed.

AGERATUM, OR FLOSS FLOWER *(Ageratum houstonianum)* – Ageratum is often combined with other plants. Indeed, this is its main purpose. It makes a marvellous edging plant, or it can be interplanted with other plants of similar size, such as wax begonias. Ageratum is a dwarf, bushy plant with powderpuff-like flowers mainly in various shades of blue. Other colours include mauve, purple, pink and white. For a lovely single-colour design combine blue ageratum with blue heliotrope, verbena or petunias.

HELIOTROPE *(Heliotropium arborescens, H. peruvianum)* – This bushy plant reaches up to 60cm (2ft) in height. The flowers come in various shades of blue, including deep violet. It combines well with many other plants such as zonal pelargoniums, salvias, petunias and marigolds. It also works well as the centrepiece for a blue design that incorporates blue petunias or lobelia.

VERBENA HYBRIDS *(Verbena* x *hybrida, V.* x *hortensis)* – These lowish, somewhat spreading plants have flowers in shades of red, pink and blue. Mixtures and separate colours are available.

AFRICAN MARIGOLDS *(Tagetes erecta)* – The large double flowers come in many shades of yellow and orange, the blooms being produced from early summer until the frosts arrive in autumn. Varieties range in height from 30–90cm (1–3ft). Separate colours and mixtures are available. The tall varieties are especially useful for giving height to designs. Yellow or orange marigolds look lovely mixed with blue heliotrope or petunias, and yellow marigolds look very nice in a single-colour design with yellow petunias.

FRENCH MARIGOLDS *(Tagetes patula)* – These dwarf plants are ideal for mass planting with other small plants like blue ageratum. The flowers come in many shades of yellow and orange, plus mahogany, and may be single or double.

ORNAMENTAL TOBACCO *(Nicotiana alata, N. affinis)* – The flowers are often fragrant and come in various colours such as red, pink and white. There is also a green variety. Mixtures as well as separate colours are available. If you want to create a white design, try white ornamental tobacco with white marguerites. They are especially recommended for cottage-garden patios.

ABOVE *Lobelia is available as bushy or trailing plants and comes in blue shades and other colours. Alternative plants for this strawberry pot include mimulus and verbenas.*

BELOW *Treasure flowers or gazanias are ideal for hot, dry, sunny situations.*

LEFT *The sun plant or portulaca is a low-growing succulent with brilliantly coloured flowers, ideally suited to hot, dry conditions. It can be grown successfully in shallow containers. The flowers of some varieties only open when the sun is shining.*

There is another verbena called *V. venosa (V. rigida)* that has a stiff, upright habit of growth up to 45cm (18in) high with heads of purple flowers. It makes an extremely useful foil for other plants such as zonal pelargoniums and scarlet salvias.

LOBELIA *(Lobelia erinus)* – Lobelia is very popular in Great Britain, but North American summers tend to be too hot for it. It is primarily used for edging containers and because it comes mainly in blue shades, it is a useful constituent of blue designs. There are both compact and trailing varieties, the latter being suitable for the edges of containers.

GOLDEN FEATHER *(Pyrethrum parthenium, Chrysanthemum parthenium)* – This is a dwarf plant with bright yellow, finely cut foliage and is an ideal edging for an all-yellow design. The white daisy flowers are usually cut off because they detract from the beauty of the foliage.

FEVERFEW *(Matricaria eximea)* – Also a dwarf, feverfew produces masses of white buttonlike flowers; it is a good choice for edging an all-white scheme.

TREASURE FLOWERS *(Gazania x hybrida)* – These are low-growing plants with large, daisy-like blooms in many bright colours. The flowers of many modern strains stay open in dull weather. For hot, dry situations there is nothing to beat these.

LIVINGSTONE DAISY *(Mesembryanthemum criniflorum)* – This has daisy flowers in jewel-like colours, which open only in the sun. Both this and treasure flower are especially suitable for shallow bowls.

The following are slightly more unusual plants that also provide summer colour in patio containers:

CELOSIA, OR PRINCE OF WALES' FEATHERS *(Celosia plumosa)* – This has feathery plumes of red, yellow or apricot flowers.

COLEUS, OR FLAME NETTLE *(Coleus blumei)* – It is a foliage plant with multicoloured leaves.

KINGFISHER DAISY *(Felicia bergerana)* – Here is a little annual with blue daisy flowers that blooms from early summer to early autumn. It is good with an edging of golden feather.

MARGUERITES *(Argyranthemum frutescens, Chrysanthemum frutescens)* – The daisylike flowers are white in the species but the varieties come in various colours.

MONKEY FLOWER *(Mimulus x hybridus)* – This is a dwarf plant with trumpet-shaped flowers in shades of red, pink, orange and yellow. It needs moist soil. Plant it in the shade in hot climates; it can be grown in sun or partial shade in temperate climates.

DWARF MORNING GLORY *(Convolvulus tricolor, C. minor)* – This low, bushy annual has blue, white-centred, trumpet-shaped flowers.

SLIPPERWORT *(Calceolaria integrifolia, C. rugosa)* – This is a bedding calceolaria that grows up to 60cm (2ft) high with bright yellow pouched flowers all summer. It is excellent for yellow designs.

STAR OF THE VELDT *(Dimorphotheca aurantiaca)* – This fairly low, spreading plant has masses of large, bright orange daisy-like flowers all summer that open only in bright and sunny weather. For a striking combination try growing it with the kingfisher daisy.

SUN PLANT *(Portulaca grandiflora)* – A low succulent plant for hot, dry conditions, the sun plant has brilliant flowers in red, pink, yellow and other colours all summer.

SWEET PEA *(Lathyrus odoratus)* – Look for the dwarf bushy varieties. They have flowers which are often fragrant in a wide range of colours that bloom all summer. They are more popular in Great Britain than in North America.

AUTUMN COLOUR

If you find that your patio is lacking colour in the autumn, or you want some additional colour for this season, you could plant some containers with dwarf chrysanthemums. These should be grown in pots in some other part of the garden and simply plunged up to their pot rims in the container soil as they are coming into flower. Alternatively garden centres generally offer pot-grown plants for immediate effect.

Suncharm chrysanthemums naturally form dwarf, compact bushes that do not need stopping or disbudding. They are smothered with small single flowers in most of the chrysanthemum colours from late summer until mid autumn.

American cushion mums produce masses of double or single flowers in a wide range of colours. These are also dwarf, bushy plants, but frequent removal of the terminal buds in the early stages of growth is recommended to achieve a good cushion shape.

ABOVE *Autumn need not be colourless as dwarf chrysanthemums and pansies will make a fine show. Dwarf bedding dahlias will still be flowering at this time of year.*

WINTER COLOUR

The only bedding plants that will provide winter colour are winter-flowering pansies (varieties of *Viola* x *wittrockiana*). There are not many strains of these, the most popular being 'Universal' and 'Floral Dance' in mixed or separate colours. These pansies are surprisingly hardy (suitable for temperatures down to −15°C/5°F), even flowering through a layer of snow. And they have an exceptionally long flowering period, continuing well into spring.

EVERGREENS FOR COLD-WINTER AREAS

It has already been stated that in areas with very cold winters (below −12°C/10°F), winter- and spring-flowering bedding plants, and bulbs, will not survive when planted in containers. However, to ensure winter and spring interest, small, very hardy evergreen shrubs could be grown in some containers, either alone or with a view to planting summer bedding plants between them. The following small evergreen shrubs are recommended.:

RED BEARBERRY *(Arctostaphyllos uva-ursi)* – This is a creeping shrub with small white flowers and red berries. It needs lime-free soil.

EUONYMUS FORTUNEI – Sometimes known as winter creeper, varieties have bushy and trailing habits with plain green or silver/gold variegated foliage. They are suitable for shade.

CHECKERBERRY *(Gaultheria procumbens)* – This is a creeping shrub with deep green foliage and bright red berries in autumn and winter. It needs lime-free soil.

ENGLISH IVY *(Hedera helix)* – This familiar ivy has a trailing habit and small, lobed leaves in plain green, variegated or gold. It is excellent for shade and is often used for trailing over the edges of containers.

ABOVE *This arrangement of conical junipers, golden thuja, variegated euonymous and ivies should winter successfully in a sheltered position.*

LEFT *Pansies can flower at any time of year, even in winter if suitable cultivars are chosen. They are ideally suited to container growing. Cut off the dead flower heads for a non-stop display.*

CREEPING JUNIPER *(Juniperus horizontalis)* – This juniper has a prostrate habit. There are numerous varieties with green or greyish foliage, sometimes flushed purple in winter. 'Bar Harbor' is one of the best, with grey-green foliage. It is suitable for shade.

LABRADOR TEA *(Ledum groenlandicum)* – This erect shrub grows up to 90cm (3ft) in height with clusters of white flowers during spring and early summer. Leaves have rust-coloured undersides. 'Compactum' is a dwarf form. It needs lime-free soil.

LONICERA PILEATA – This is a spreading semi-evergreen shrub with tiny bright green leaves and translucent violet berries. It is an excellent shrub for shade.

OREGON GRAPE *(Mahonia aquifolium)* – Suitable for partial shade, this shrub has pinnate leaves that are red-flushed in winter. Clusters of deep yellow flowers appear in early spring and these are followed by bunches of blue-black berries. It grows to a height of about 90cm (3ft).

JAPANESE SPURGE *(Pachysandra terminalis)* – This is a low carpeting plant with clusters of somewhat diamond-shaped leaves and spikes of tiny green-white flowers in late winter or early spring. It thrives in shade and likes steadily moist soil. There is an attractive white-variegated variety called 'Variegata'.

PERNETTYA MUCRONATA – This dwarf shrub is good for moist, peaty, lime-free soils, producing white flowers in spring followed by clusters of large, rounded berries in shades of red, pink and white. A male needs to be planted among female plants to ensure berry production. Although this shrub will tolerate cold conditions, it is not recommended for areas where the winters are extremely severe, and temperatures drop below −18°C/0°F.

JAPANESE YEW *(Taxus cuspidata)* – Dwarf varieties such as 'Densa' have a dense, mounded habit; 'Minima' is very slow growing and of informal outline; and 'Nana' is a very dense bush. These are much hardier than the varieties of the better-known English yew (*T. baccata*).

CANADA HEMLOCK *(Tsuga canadensis)* – Dwarf varieties such as 'Compacta' have a very dense, conical habit; 'Globosa' is a very compact globe-shaped bush; and 'Nana' has a low spreading habit and is slow growing.

PERMANENT PLANTS

If you don't want to go to all the trouble of changing bedding plants several times a year as weather and blooming times change, you can use permanent plants instead. Many shrubs, small trees, climbers, roses and hardy perennials do well in patio containers. Recommended sizes of tubs for permanent plants have already been given. Many people prefer to use a potting soil that contains loam, peat and sand for permanent plants, although peat-based soils are also good. However, peat-based soils are not dense enough for large shrubs and small trees and usually cannot give these larger plants the strong anchor they need.

SHRUBS

The best times to plant evergreen shrubs are mid spring and early autumn. Deciduous kinds may be planted in autumn or early spring. Bear in mind that many of the fol-

LEFT *Mop-headed hydrangeas need a moisture-retentive soil and flourish in partial shade or full sun.*

ABOVE *Rhododendrons, ideally dwarf kinds, are suitable for growing in containers; they flower in the spring. They need lime-free soil, which makes them ideal for containers if the soil in your garden tends to be alkaline.*

lowing will not withstand very severe winters (below −12°C/10°F) in containers, unless protected in some way. A list of small, tougher evergreen shrubs suitable for colder areas can be found on page 31.

JAPANESE MAPLE *(Acer palmatum)* – Many cultivars produce brilliant autumn leaf colour. Others have red foliage in spring and summer. It is best in lime-free soil and in a sheltered position.

BARBERRY *(Berberis* x *stenophylla)* – This evergreen spiny shrub has deep yellow flowers in mid spring. It makes a good background for a group of containers.

FAR LEFT *The box (*Buxus sempervirens*) is an evergreen shrub suitable for shade and can be trained to a formal shape if desired.*

LEFT *Japanese fatsia (*Fatsia japonica*) is an excellent 'architectural' background plant for sun or shade. Its exotic appearance contrasts dramatically with the rest of the garden.*

Box *(Buxus sempervirens)* – Suitable for shade, this evergreen has small leaves and is usually grown as a formal clipped specimen, including topiary.

CAMELLIA – This evergreen shrub has handsome glossy foliage and pink, red or white flowers in winter and spring. Use cultivars of *C. japonica* or *C.* x *williamsii.* It needs a lime-free soil and a position out of early morning sun. It is suitable for shade.

LAWSON CYPRESS *(Chamaecyparis lawson-iana)* – The conical cultivars 'Ellwoodii' (grey-green) and 'Ellwood's Gold' (tinged yellow) of this evergreen conifer are suitable for tubs.

MEXICAN ORANGE BLOSSOM *(Choisya ternata)* – This is a tender evergreen that is best overwintered under glass in cold areas. There are white, highly fragrant flowers in spring and early summer.

DAPHNE ODORA 'AUREOMARGINATA' – This small evergreen shrub has highly fragrant

LEFT *Container-grown Japanese maple (*Acer palmatum*). It needs a sheltered position and lime-free soil.*

purple-pink flowers in winter and spring, and cream-edged leaves. It is best over-wintered under glass in cold areas.

ELAEAGNUS PUNGENS 'MACULATA' – Excellent as a background plant and very bright in winter, this evergreen has bright gold-splashed leaves.

ESCALLONIA – There are many species and cultivars of these tender evergreen shrubs producing pink, red or white flowers in summer. It is recommended only for mild climates.

JAPANESE SPINDLE TREE (Euonymus japonicus) – This evergreen has shiny green leaves. More attractive are the white or yellow variegated cultivars. It thrives in shade.

JAPANESE FATSIA (Fatsia japonica) – An excellent 'architectural' background plant with its large hand-shaped leaves, it needs wintering under glass in cold areas. It is suitable for shade.

GOLDEN BELLS (Forsythia x intermedia 'Lynwood') – The branches are completely covered with large, bright yellow flowers in early spring. It is excellent as a background for spring bulbs but is uninteresting for the rest of the year.

FUCHSIA MAGELLANICA – Normally cultivars are grown, with bell-shaped flowers mainly in scarlet and violet during the summer. This is a tender plant, so winter under glass in cold areas. It tolerates partial shade.

HEATHERS – These are dwarf evergreen shrubs suitable for various seasons, with flowers in various shades. Cultivars of *Calluna vulgaris* flower in summer or autumn. Some have coloured foliage. For winter through to spring grow cultivars of *Erica herbacea (E. carnea)* and *E. x darleyensis.* Lime-free soil is needed.

SHRUBBY VERONICA (Hebe) – This evergreen shrub has spikes of flowers in shades of blue, purple, red or white in summer and early autumn. Many are tender and recommended only for mild areas.

HYDRANGEA MACROPHYLLA – Flowering in summer and autumn, the mop-headed cultivars have large globular heads of blooms, and the lacecap kinds have flat flower heads. They come in shades of red, pink and blue, plus white. Give it moisture-retentive soil and full sun or partial shade.

ABOVE *Lawson cypress* (Chamaecyparis lawsoniana) *is suited to tub culture and may if desired be grown as a mop-headed standard. The tradition of flanking steps with standards is still popular.*

Heathers are dwarf evergreen shrubs suitable for various seasons with flowers in shades of pink, red, purple, lilac and white. They should be grown in lime-free soil. Trim lightly with shears after flowering to remove dead blooms. Heathers can be used as ground cover around trees or large shrubs provided they are not shaded.

OPPOSITE TOP *A mop-headed standard privet is complemented by crocuses planted around the base. Shrubby veronicas or hebes are evergreen shrubs which flower in the summer and some have variegated foliage (RIGHT). They are recommended only for mild areas.*

OPPOSITE BOTTOM *Some mop-headed hydrangeas have beautiful blue flowers but unless grown in acid or lime-free soil they will turn pink. Remove dead flowers in spring.*

ENGLISH HOLLY *(Ilex aquifolium)* – This prickly evergreen is best in its variegated cultivars such as 'Argentea Marginata'. It can be grown naturally or as formal clipped specimens. It is excellent for shade.

JUNIPER *(Juniperus)* – Many of these evergreen conifers are suitable for containers, such as Irish juniper *(J. communis* 'Hibernica'), of dense columnar habit, and creeping juniper *(J. horizontalis),* with cultivars that have a spreading prostrate or low habit. All are suitable for shade.

SWEET BAY *(Laurus nobilis)* – This evergreen with aromatic foliage has a pyramidal habit but is normally clipped. It is only recommended for mild areas.

MAHONIA JAPONICA – This is an 'architectural' shrub with large, evergreen, pinnate leaves. Long trusses of fragrant yellow flowers are produced between late autumn and early spring. It thrives only in mild areas. Although it is suitable for partial shade this plant needs to be sheltered from cold winds. It associates beautifully with architecture and paving.

MAGNOLIA – Two are suitable for containers: star magnolia *(M. stellata)*, with white starry flowers on bare branches in early to mid spring, and *M.* x *soulangiana* cultivars, with large goblet-shaped flowers in white, usually flushed purple, during mid spring before the leaves appear. The latter is best in lime-free soil.

MOUNTAIN PINE *(Pinus mugo pumilio)* – This is a dwarf, bushy evergreen pine with a somewhat prostrate habit. The foliage is deep green. It is excellent for including in groups of heathers for contrast in shape and texture.

RHODODENDRON – Any dwarf rhododendron is suitable for growing in containers. Most flower in spring and come in a wide range of colours. Almost all are evergreen. Dwarf evergreen azaleas are also highly recommended, producing a mass of flowers in mid- to late spring in various shades of pink and red, also white. All rhododendrons thrive in partial shade and must have lime-free soil.

Rhododendron yakushimanum is rather special, being considered by many

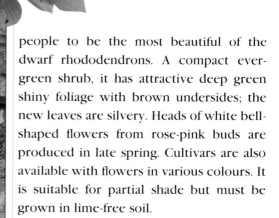

people to be the most beautiful of the dwarf rhododendrons. A compact evergreen shrub, it has attractive deep green shiny foliage with brown undersides; the new leaves are silvery. Heads of white bell-shaped flowers from rose-pink buds are produced in late spring. Cultivars are also available with flowers in various colours. It is suitable for partial shade but must be grown in lime-free soil.

IRISH YEW *(Taxus baccata* 'Fastigiata') – This popular evergreen conifer has an upright, columnar habit of growth and very deep green foliage. It is useful for creating

*The sweet bay (*Laurus nobilis*) is an evergreen shrub which can be trained to various shapes although it is recommended for mild areas only. It is of course useful as a fresh herb.*

a formal effect on patios. A pair would be ideal for 'framing' a doorway. It is a suitable choice for a shady position.

LAURUSTINUS *(Viburnum tinus)* – This extremely useful evergreen shrub produces heads of white flowers between late autumn and mid spring, so it is a natural choice for winter and spring groups on the patio. During summer the deep green foliage makes an excellent background for colourful summer bedding plants. There are several cultivars including 'Lucidum', with larger leaves and flower heads. This blooms in the spring. 'Variegatum' has cream-variegated foliage.

YUCCA – The yuccas are 'architectural' plants with sword-shaped leaves, and bold spikes of white or cream lily-like flowers in summer on established plants. They are ideal for creating an exotic touch on a patio, perhaps in association with phormiums and kniphofias (see the section Hardy Perennials later in this chapter). They also look good in association with brightly coloured summer bedding plants such as pelargoniums. The yuccas revel in hot conditions. There are numerous species including the popular Adam's needle *(Y. gloriosa)*. Dwarf yuccas include *Y. filamentosa,* which has white threads along the edges of the leaves.

SMALL TREES

Many people do not realize that several small trees adapt happily to life in containers. They are especially useful on the patio for creating additional height to plant groups, and most produce dappled shade which may be appreciated during hot weather.

For stability, small trees are best grown in soil that contains loam, peat and sand. The weight of such soil will prevent the trees from being blown over during windy weather. Plant in autumn or early spring.

ENGLISH HAWTHORN *(Crataegus laevigata, C. oxyacantha)* – This is a round-headed tree that flowers profusely in late spring. Normally cultivars are grown such as 'Coccinea Plena' ('Paulii'), with double scarlet blossoms; 'Plena', with double white blossoms; and 'Rosea', with single bright pink blooms. All are tolerant of cold, exposed conditions.

JAPANESE CRAB *(Malus floribunda)* – This is a most attractive, very hardy tree with long branches that arch over. In mid- to late spring these are wreathed with white or palest pink blossoms from deep red buds. They are followed by small yellow and red fruits. When these fall they should be promptly swept up, otherwise they may get crushed and stain the paving.

WEEPING WILLOW-LEAVED PEAR *(Pyrus salicifolia* 'Pendula') – This small weeping tree has narrow, willow-like, silvery leaves. As it becomes established cream-white flowers are produced, followed by brown,

inedible fruits. However, the tree is essentially grown for its foliage, which makes a good background for brightly coloured summer bedding plants such as orange pelargoniums.

FALSE ACACIA *(Robinia pseudoacacia* 'Frisia') – This is among the brightest of all small trees, associating particularly well with modern architecture and paving. Nothing is better for brightening up areas of dull concrete. The ferny leaves are deep yellow from spring to autumn. It tolerates hot, dry conditions and atmospheric pollution and so is ideally suited to towns and cities.

KILMARNOCK WILLOW *(Salix caprea* 'Pendula', *S.c.* 'Kilmarnock') – This is a small willow whose branches are pendulous yet stiffly held. It makes an excellent specimen plant for the patio. Grey then yellow catkins are produced from early to mid spring. It is very hardy and adaptable.

ROWAN OR MOUNTAIN ASH *(Sorbus aucuparia* 'Fastigiata') – This small, extremely

ABOVE *Hollies can be grown as shrubs or trees and are amenable to training into various shapes such as the popular mop-headed standard.*

hardy, wind-resistant tree has a narrow up-right habit, so it takes up little space. It is no good for producing shade, though! It has deep green pinnate foliage and clusters of rich red berries in autumn. These will stain paving, so they should be carefully swept up as soon as they fall. It makes an excellent focal point and could also form the centrepiece of a group of shrubs.

CLIMBERS

Invariably there are walls adjacent to patios, perhaps to help provide shelter from cold winds, or maybe there is just a wall of the house. Such vertical space is often ideal for growing climbers.

Climbers are attractive plants in their own right, but they also make good backgrounds for other plants. The more vigorous kinds will not take too kindly to being restricted in patio containers. On the other hand, there are several of a more restrained habit that will settle down happily to life in a tub. As with small ornamental trees, climbers are best grown in potting soil consisting of loam, peat and sand. They can be planted in autumn or early spring.

VIRGIN'S BOWER (*Clematis*) – Some of these are extremely vigorous climbers and are not good for container growing. However, the large-flowered garden hybrids are more restrained and take perfectly to containers. Most flower in summer. Choose from such well-known cultivars as 'Jackmanii Superba', deep violet-purple; 'Lasurstern', deep lavender blue; and 'Nelly Moser', light mauve-pink with a red bar to each petal. Clematis like cool roots, so keep their bottoms shaded with, for example, dwarf shrubs. But they like their heads in the sun so don't plant in the shade. Clematis like alkaline soil. The large-flowered clematis make excellent companions for climbing roses; allow them to intertwine.

IVY (*Hedera*) – These are evergreen climbers that make an excellent background for other plants. Some have comparatively large, bold leaves, such as Persian ivy (*Hedera colchica*) and Canary Island ivy (*H. canariensis*). They have plain green leaves, but there are variegated forms of each that are more widely grown. They are not recommended for areas subjected to hard winters. Tougher is English ivy (*H.*

white jasmine that produces masses of highly fragrant flowers from early summer to early autumn. This makes an attractive companion for red or pink climbing roses. Both are reasonably hardy, withstanding moderately hard winters.

EARLY DUTCH HONEYSUCKLE (*Lonicera periclymenum* 'Belgica') – This climber is valued for its fragrant flowers that are heavily flushed with red-purple on the outside, eventually changing to yellow. These are produced in late spring and early summer but invariably there is a second flush at the end of summer. It tolerates partial shade.

EUROPEAN GRAPE (*Vitis vinifera* 'Purpurea') – This is an ornamental grape with claret-red young foliage that later turns deep purple. It looks lovely planted with red climbing roses.

ABOVE *Clematis montana is a vigorous spring-flowering species. Although not generally recommended for container growing, it will flourish in a very large pot or tub.*

helix), of which there are many cultivars with both plain green, often deeply lobed and cut, and variegated foliage. Widely grown is the Irish ivy (*H. helix* 'Hibernica'), with deep green lobed leaves larger than those of the species. It makes an excellent background plant.

JASMINE, JESSAMINE (*Jasminum*) – There are two useful species for container growing. For winter colour try *J. nudiflorum,* which bears bright yellow starry flowers on bare stems between late autumn and late winter. It is suitable for a shady wall. *J. officinale* is the common

ROSES

There are few permanent plants that provide so much summer colour as roses. They bloom from early summer and into autumn. The smaller kinds adapt readily to containers and are very hardy, but may need some winter protection in colder climates. Grow in a potting soil that contains loam, peat and sand, and plant in autumn or early spring.

FLORIBUNDA ROSES – These are excellent for containers, as they have clusters of small flowers in a wide colour range. Choose the low-growing cultivars.

MINIATURE ROSES – These are now extremely popular and ideal for tiny patios where they will be more in scale compared to, for example, floribundas. There

ABOVE *It is best to choose small-growing cultivars of climbing roses for containers, ideally with several flushes of blooms in summer. They flower most freely in a sunny position and need feeding in spring and summer.*

LEFT *Miniature roses are ideal for tiny patios and there are hundreds of cultivars to choose from. These can be combined with small silver or grey foliage plants.*

are hundreds of cultivars in a wide colour range, so choose those that you find most appealing. Miniatures are under 45cm (18in) high.

CLIMBING ROSES – It is best to choose small-growing cultivars of climbing roses for containers, avoiding the very vigorous kinds. And choose those that produce several flushes of blooms during the summer, rather than a single display. There are many to choose from, in a wide range of colours.

HARDY PERENNIALS

These are often grouped with shrubs to create contrast in shape, texture and colour. Many perennials will not flower or grow well in containers, so they have to be chosen carefully. Those described here are known from experience to adapt readily to life in containers.

Hardy perennials are best grown in a well-drained soil containing loam, peat and sand, but all-peat soils are also suitable. Best planting time is early spring. Remember that most perennials die down for the winter and then contribute nothing until next summer or perhaps late spring. The dead growth should be cut down to soil level in the autumn. If grown in their own containers they can then be moved to another part of the garden where hopefully they will be hidden from view.

AFRICAN LILY (*Agapanthus orientalis*) – This is a half-hardy evergreen perennial with strap-shaped leaves and heads of blue funnel-shaped flowers in summer. There are also white forms. It is on the tender side and except in areas with mild winters is best wintered in a frost-free greenhouse. It grows well in large tubs and looks particularly attractive in terracotta containers. Given regular feeds, plants can remain undisturbed for several years.

BELOW *African lily (Agapanthus orientalis) is a half-hardy summer-flowering evergreen perennial but is well suited to container growing. It is best wintered in a frost-free greenhouse except in very mild areas.*

ABOVE *Plantain lilies or hostas are dramatic foliage plants which contrast superbly with many shrubs (including hydrangeas) and perennials. In summer they produce lilac or white lily-like flowers. They are excellent for shady spots, needing constantly moist soil.*

HELICTOTRICHON SEMPERVIRENS – This is an ornamental grass forming clumps of bluish foliage that contrasts superbly with many other perennials and shrubs, especially those with large, rounded leaves. Many other small ornamental grasses may also be grown in containers.

HELLEBORUS ARGUTIFOLIUS – Also known as *H. corsicus* and *H. lividus corsicus,* this is an evergreen perennial with attractive, three-lobed, light green, spiny leaves. In early to mid spring it has heads of yellowish green, bowl-shaped flowers. An excellent 'architectural' plant for partial shade, it is pleasing with spring-flowering shrubs.

PLANTAIN LILY (*Hosta*) – These days hostas are 'essential' perennials for many situations, the large leaves in every shade of green, plus 'blue', grey, yellow and variegated, contrasting superbly with shrubs and perennials. In summer these low-growing, very hardy plants produce spikes of small, lilylike flowers in shades of lilac, mauve, purple or white. There are many species and cultivars to choose from. They are superb for shady spots, needing constantly moist soil.

LADY'S MANTLE (*Alchemilla mollis*) – This low-growing perennial is attractive in all its parts, with pale green lobed leaves and frothy yellowish green flowers throughout summer. It is often used as a contrast for other plants and associates particularly well with shrubs of all kinds.

SPURGE (*Euphorbia wulfenii*) – This is an 'architectural' plant that associates well with modern architecture and paving, as well as with shrubs of all kinds. It is evergreen with blue-green, lance-shaped leaves and in summer bears large heads of tiny flowers surrounded by conspicuous yellow-green bracts.

TORCH LILY, OR RED-HOT POKER (*Kniphofia caulescens*) – This is one of the most dramatic of the torch lilies, with broad, grassy, evergreen, grey-green foliage and in summer bold spikes of light red flowers. It must be wintered under glass except in very mild climates. It needs very well-drained soil and can be left undisturbed for many years when grown in a tub.

MONEYWORT, OR CREEPING JENNY (*Lysimachia nummularia*) – This is a creeping evergreen perennial with rounded leaves and yellow, cup-shaped flowers in summer. The cultivar 'Aurea' has yellow foliage. It is useful for trailing over the edges of containers and may be planted around shrubs. It is suited to moisture-retentive or dry soils and tolerates partial shade.

NEW ZEALAND FLAX (*Phormium tenax*) – This half-hardy evergreen perennial has long, upright, sword-shaped leaves, giving an exotic touch to a patio. There are numerous cultivars, including the bronze-purple 'Purpureum' and green and yellow striped 'Variegatum'. Many very colourful cultivars have been produced in New Zealand. In cold climates (below −6°C/20°F) winter the plants in a cool greenhouse.

RODGERSIA PINNATA – This 'architectural' perennial is grown mainly for its foliage, which looks good with modern architecture and paving. The large, hand-shaped leaves are dark green but may be flushed with bronze. However the leaves are not the only attractive feature: plumes of pink flowers are produced in the summertime. This plant needs moist soil and partial shade, as well as shelter from the wind.

ABOVE *There are numerous cultivars of New Zealand flax* (Phormium tenax) *with bold sword-shaped leaves in various colours. This perennial is half-hardy and in cold climates will need wintering in a cool greenhouse.*

2

Window Boxes

It probably comes as a surprise to learn that window boxes have been used for growing plants since Roman times. These were undoubtedly earthenware containers, but since then many other materials have been used for making them. In Medieval Europe, for instance, window boxes were made from wattle or strips of wood woven together, as well as from metal, and again clay, especially terracotta.

CHOOSING BOXES

Today it is possible to buy window boxes in various materials. Terracotta is still used, and these boxes look very nice, too, especially on older-style properties, including country houses. They often have ornate relief designs. But there is one drawback with terracotta window boxes. Being porous, the soil is inclined to dry out rapidly during warm weather.

In the past lead window boxes were popular, and today it is still possible to buy them in this material, generally in traditional styles, because these look most 'comfortable' when installed in period homes. Although most lead window boxes are not large, they are expensive and, of course, very heavy.

Many window boxes today are made from plastic and come in various sizes, colours and styles. Plastic is more suitable for modern settings and has the advantage of being lightweight and therefore easy to handle. Because plastic is non-porous, the soil in such boxes dries out less quickly than in, for example, terracotta boxes.

Wooden window boxes are very popular today, due to a great extent to the many styles and finishes in which they are available. There are modern styles in wood to suit contemporary houses, traditional styles for traditional homes, and more rustic boxes for country houses.

The insides of wooden window boxes should be treated every two years with a horticultural wood preservative to prevent rotting. Never use a non-horticultural preservative; you could damage plants if you do. The outsides of boxes can be similarly treated if you want a natural wood finish. You could choose a coloured wood preservative, such as dark oak or teak, or use a clear preservative. Alternatively wooden window boxes can be painted on the outside to coordinate with the building.

OPPOSITE *Window boxes are available in various materials so it is comparatively easy to match them with the house decor. A cluttered background calls for plants in a single bold colour.*

LEFT *Today the trend is for simple designs using few colours. This combination of cream, pink, blue and grey plants is very tasteful and suitable for the style of the house.*

BELOW *Terracotta window boxes are popular and an appropriate choice for older-style properties, although they should also be considered for modern homes.*

INSTALLING BOXES

Care should be taken when installing window boxes. When filled with plants and soil and then watered, even lightweight plastic boxes are going to be heavy. They must be firmly secured.

If the windowsill is wide enough to accommodate the box without it overhanging then all you need do is fix the box to the window frame or the wall with screws. If the window sill slopes forward, as many do to shed rainwater, then you will need to place wooden wedges under the front of the box to make it level.

If you have narrow window sills, the boxes will most likely overhang the edges. However, you can still put boxes on them, provided you support them underneath with strong metal brackets of suitable size that are fixed to the wall and to the base of the window box. Generally a bracket at each end of a box is sufficient. If your boxes are in a prominent spot you may want to choose decorative brackets, per-

haps in fancy wrought iron. Or you could go with something plain and paint them to match the boxes.

Window boxes must have holes in their bases to allow excess water to drain away. In some cases the resultant drips could be a problem unless shallow plastic drip trays are placed under the boxes when they are installed and you are careful not to overwater.

MAKING YOUR OWN BOXES

Anyone handy with carpenters' tools can easily make wooden window boxes. The advantages here are that not only can you make them of a practical depth to prevent rapid drying out (some ready-made ones are inclined to be on the shallow side), but you can also construct them to exactly fit your window sills.

The best woods for outdoor use are redwood, teak and western red cedar. These are expensive; cheaper is fir, which will last many years if regularly treated with preservative. Any wood used should be 1.9–2.5cm (¾–1in) thick.

To prevent rapid drying out of the soil make boxes 25–30cm (10–12in) deep. To create well-proportioned boxes make them as wide as they are deep.

If your windowsills are very long, do not make one long window box to fit the space because it will be heavy and difficult to handle. Rather, opt for several smaller ones to fit the length of the sill. For instance, if the window is 1.8m (6ft) long, make two 90cm (3ft) long boxes.

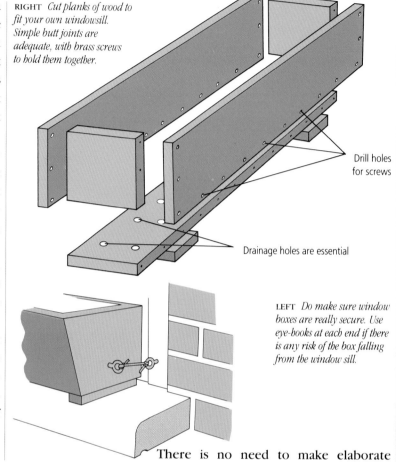

RIGHT Cut planks of wood to fit your own windowsill. Simple butt joints are adequate, with brass screws to hold them together.

Drill holes for screws

Drainage holes are essential

LEFT Do make sure window boxes are really secure. Use eye-hooks at each end if there is any risk of the box falling from the window sill.

LEFT A collection of liners or plastic troughs which fit inside window boxes allows you to change displays easily and quickly.

There is no need to make elaborate carpenters' joints when building window boxes – simple butt joints will do. Use brass screws of adequate length. If you want extra strength, screw some metal angle brackets on the inside at the corners of the box and where the base joins the sides.

Do not forget to make drainage holes in the base, about 2.5cm (1in) in diameter and 10–15cm (4–6in) apart. Fix two strips of wood, about 2.5 by 2.5cm (1 by 1in), on the underside, one at each end, to slightly raise the box off the windowsill and therefore ensure unimpeded drainage of surplus water.

Finally, treat the inside with two coats of horticultural wood preservative. Then treat the outside with preservative, or paint it.

PREPARING FOR PLANTING

Before adding soil place a 2.5cm (1in) deep layer of pebbles in the bottom of the window box to help with drainage. If possible, cover this with a thin layer of rough peat or partially rotted leaves to prevent it becoming blocked with soil. Then fill with soil to within 2.5cm (1in) of the top of the box. For temporary bedding plants many people use an all-peat potting soil. For permanent plants a potting soil containing loam, peat and sand may give better growth.

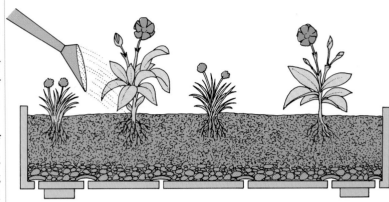

ABOVE *A window box must have drainage holes in the base which are covered with a layer of pebbles. All-peat potting soil is suitable for temporary plants, a loam-based one for permanent residents. Always water in newly planted specimens to settle the soil around them.*

LEFT *A riot of colours is more appropriate for the traditional English cottage style of garden and needs a plain uncluttered background.*

ARRANGING PLANTS EFFECTIVELY

A window box, being long and narrow, is not the easiest shape to plant effectively. Some people make the mistake of planting a single subject and setting the plants in a row. Try to avoid this: it will look too regimented and unimaginative. Aim for more shape in the design by using a mixture of plants of varying sizes and habits.

How much a window box is covered by plants should be determined by the box itself. If it is highly attractive, then it will be a pleasing feature in its own right and should not be covered by plant growth. However, a plain box is best covered with trailing plants.

There are various ways of arranging plants in window boxes. You could go for the pyramidal design: the tallest plants are set in the middle, with shorter and shorter plants grading down to each end. The ends and the front could be planted with trailers if desired.

However, if you feel that tall plants in the middle reduce light inside the house, then place the tallest plants at each end of the box and have lower-growing plants in the middle. Trailers could be set in front of the low growers.

You can place window boxes on both sunny and shady windowsills, for remember that there are temporary and permanent plants that like both kinds of light conditions. If the area is prone to wind, it is best to avoid trailing plants, for these will be lashed around and damaged. Go for sturdy, bushy subjects.

Many people do not take backgrounds into account when creating planting designs. Windows can make rather cluttered backgrounds: there is the framework, probably curtains, and maybe ornaments and pot plants on the windowsills indoors. In this situation go for simple designs outside. For

instance, choose single-colour designs that show up better than mixed colours.

If the background is plain and uncluttered then by all means use mixed colours if you wish. You may wish to keep in mind, though, that single-colour designs, coordinated with the house, are quite popular today, especially in contemporary settings. A riot of colours is more appropriate for the traditional English cottage style of garden which is enjoying renewed popularity on both sides of the Atlantic.

Do not be pressured into thinking that very complicated designs are necessary for window boxes. Certainly one does see some very elaborate arrangements, and it's easy to get carried away by the wide range of colourful bedding plants available at garden centres. But often the use of too many different plants creates a fussy, uneasy appearance. Instead, consider comparatively simple designs, using perhaps two or three different kinds of plants.

LINERS FOR QUICK CHANGES

Fresh, vibrant seasonal flowers look lovely in window boxes, but to keep them looking at their best usually means removing plants that have finished flowering and replacing them with more plants in full bloom. This takes good planning and special effort. One

ABOVE *Compact bushy plants are suitable for bow window boxes. These yellow and white pansies are very effective against the green shutters: a simple yet very effective design which can be achieved in summer or winter.*

ABOVE *The white marguerites create height while the blue, yellow and orange pansies give a sense of depth.*

way to make the job more manageable is to grow plants in window-box liners.

A liner is simply a plastic trough of suitable size that fits inside the window box. It should have drainage holes in the base. It is best to devote a spare part of the garden to liners, to have a place where they can be planted and stored.

For instance, you can plant some with young dwarf chrysanthemums in the spring and grow them there throughout summer. Then, as they are coming into flower in the autumn, you can put the liner with its blooming plants in the window box to replace fading summer bedding plants. Or, in autumn plant some liners with winter-flowering pansies and when these come into full bloom place them in window boxes to replace autumn flowers. Spring-flowering bulbs can be planted in the autumn and kept in a spare part of the garden, or under cover and protected from frost if winters are cold, until they are ready to flower. Some liners could be planted with perm-anent plants, such as dwarf conifers and heathers, and these could be used to fill any gaps between flowering periods, which will most likely be during late autumn or early winter.

COLOUR FROM SEASONAL PLANTS

As with patio containers, spring and summer bedding plants, spring bulbs and other temporary specimens can make very colourful window boxes. Also as with other containers, a few permanent plants can be arranged in window boxes with bedding plants or bulbs planted around them. This gives variation, particularly in shape and texture. One can use dwarf conifers and small evergreen shrubs, a selection of which has been described on pages 33–38.

The choice of bedding plants and bulbs for window boxes is the same as for patio containers (see pages 22–31), with a few additions and deletions. Obviously one would not use very tall plants like Indian shot and castor oil plants in window boxes.

With window boxes it is important to consider designs for both sunny and shady positions, for some parts of the house will be bathed in sunshine all day long and other parts will receive little or none. Sun-loving plants will grow poorly and produce few flowers in shady positions. However, all of these recommended here for shade will also grow in sunny locations.

PLANTING DESIGNS FOR SUN

There are plenty of summer designs for sunny positions. The pelargoniums really flower their heads off in sun, and for window boxes there are no finer kinds than the Swiss balcony 'geraniums' that provide cascades of blooms all summer. These are the ones that provide much of the summer colour on balconies in Switzerland and Austria. They are actually varieties of ivy-leaf pelargonium (*P. peltatum*). The Swiss kinds are so vigorous and floriferous that no other plants are needed with them.

Ordinary varieties of ivy-leaf pelargonium can also be used in window boxes, but as

trailers in the front. They look good with bushy heliotrope (*Heliotropium arborescens, H. peruvianum*), which can be used to give height, and with the lower-growing blue ageratum.

Trailing petunias are marvellous plants for window boxes; allow them to cascade over the front. They go well with the bushy zonal pelargoniums. Try orange pelargoniums with blue or purple petunias for a bold effect.

Excellent for providing a summer display are marguerites (varieties of *Argyranthemum frutescens* or *Chrysanthemum frutescens*). The species is a bushy, tender perennial that produces masses of white daisy flowers throughout summer. There is also a range of new cultivars in various colours. Marguerites could form the main planting, but for cascading over the edge of the box try *Helichrysum petiolatum*, with its grey foliage.

African marigolds (*Tagetus erecta*) also revel in the sun and make good companions for marguerites. Tallish marigolds could be used to create height. Single-colour designs are possible with these two plants.

PLANTING DESIGNS FOR SHADE

For spring, first plant a few small shrubs (which can be left in place until they become too large) like variegated *Euonymus fortunei* and the spotted laurel (*Aucuba japonica* 'Variegata'). These could form the middle of the design or could be planted

ABOVE *A pleasing arrangement of plants, which is attractive even before the plants start flowering. A tall fuschsia at one end provides height and lower-growing zonal pelargoniums and fuchsias in the rest of the box have been chosen to avoid cutting out light to the room. Trailing plants, including ivy-leaved pelargoniums, complete the design.*

at each end of a box. Then add spring-flowering polyanthus or the more modern coloured forms of primrose.

Or try spring-flowering bulbs like small daffodils, grape hyacinths and scillas growing through a carpet of small-leaved ivy (*Hedera helix* cultivars), which would also cascade over the sides. The ivy can be left permanently in place if desired.

A beautiful summer design for shade features impatiens, or busy lizzie, the type specially bred for bedding. Contrasting with this could be some spider plants (*Chlorophytum comosum* 'Variegatum') with green and white striped grassy foliage. These could be planted near the edges so that they arch over the sides. Spider plants can be kept from year to year, but winter them indoors. To create height in the design, plant some tallish silver-leaved cineraria. You could create a green and white design by using white impatiens.

Another popular summer design for shade features pendulous tuberous begonias *Begonia* x *tuberhybrida* (Pendula group) in various colours. These have to be potted and started into growth in a greenhouse early in the year. They should be planted near the edge of the window box so that they cascade over the side. Use some young plants of the yellow-variegated abutilon (*A.*

striatum 'Thompsonii') to give height. (The abutilon can be kept in a frost-free greenhouse over winter but will eventually grow too tall for the window box.) By using yellow begonias you will have a pleasing yellow scheme.

Trailing fuchsias are excellent for shady summer window boxes. Plant them near the edges and create height with a bush fuchsia or two. Spider plants make a superb contrast in shape and colour. Alternatively try fresh green asparagus ferns (*Asparagus densiflorus* 'Sprengeri') with fuchsias — they will arch over the edge of the box. Keep these from year to year, but winter them indoors.

Many people do not think of using the trailing bellflower (*Campanula isophylla*) outdoors, but it certainly will survive the summer, producing cascades of blue and white flowers. Plant it near the front edge of the box for maximum effect. A trailing foliage plant that contrasts effectively with this bellflower is the white-variegated ground ivy (*Glechoma hederacea* 'Variegata'), a hardy perennial. For height in this design use a small plant of New Zealand cabbage palm.

Hopefully these few ideas for designs in shade will inspire you and lead to other designs.

PERMANENT PLANTING DESIGNS

If you do not want to go to all the trouble of regularly changing planting designs, choose permanent designs instead. Alternatively, you may find some permanent arrangements that you planted in liners useful for filling in gaps between flowering periods. For instance, there may be a gap between spring and summer or autumn winter bedding. See the section called 'Liners for Quick Changes' on page 51.

FOR SUNNY POSITIONS

Miniature roses, which are becoming incredibly popular today, are very nice for summer-long colour in window boxes. Try planting small silver- or grey-foliage plants with them, such as the cotton lavender (*Santolina chamaecyparisus* 'Nana') or the lavenders *Lavandula angustifolia* 'Munstead' or *L. lanata.*

Superb designs can be created with dwarf conifers and heathers. To give height try a group of *Juniperus communis* 'Compressa', a neat, conical juniper with greyish foliage, and surround this with heathers for summer, autumn or winter colour.

Other suitable plants for sun include any of the small, shrubby veronicas or hebes, which unfortunately are not the hardiest of plants and may not survive winters in cold climates unless taken under glass. Most flower profusely in summer. Dwarf kinds include *H. albicans,* with white flowers; *H. macrantha,* also white; and *H. pinguifolia* 'Pagei', with grey foliage and white flowers. Try planting miniature spring bulbs between them, such as crocuses, grape hyacinth (muscari), glory of the snow (chionodoxa) and squills (scilla). Autumn crocuses would extend the flowering season still further.

Small culinary herbs are excellent for window boxes, if you can give them a position in full sun. A sunny kitchen windowsill would be the best place for the box because it would be so handy for the cook. Herbs are described in Chapter 6.

FOR SHADY POSITIONS

There are numerous small shrubs suitable for shade and some are described on pages 33–38. An excellent idea is to plant a collection of small shrubs in the boxes for interest at various seasons and to interplant them with small, shade-loving, spring-flowering bulbs like dwarf and miniature daffodil species and cultivars (of which there is a very wide range available) and snowdrops

(galanthus). It is best to buy and plant snow-drops immediately after flowering while they are still in leaf, as dry bulbs planted in autumn take several years to settle down and flower well.

A design which I particularly like consists of *Skimmia reevesiana,* a small evergreen shrub whose white spring blooms are followed by red berries that last all winter, with an edging of the trailing *Lysimachia nummularia* 'Aurea', with its yellow foliage, and the lesser periwinkle *(Vinca minor),* which has starry blue flowers in spring. A sprinkling of small spring bulbs can be recommended, too. Unfortunately the skimmia is not a very hardy shrub and is best suited to milder areas (−12°C/10°F and above).

Not many people consider dwarf evergreen hybrid azaleas (rhododendron) for window boxes, but they are ideal for areas in partial shade. They have a low spreading habit and in spring smother themselves with flowers in shades of red or pink, plus white. Lime-free soil that is kept constantly moist is needed. Plant some dwarf lilies between them for summer colour.

ABOVE *The predominantly white background provides a good foil for these scarlet and purple pelargoniums and petunias, two of the most popular summer-flowering annuals for window boxes.*

3

Baskets and Wall Pots

Hanging baskets and wall-mounted pots provide you with more opportunities for creating colourful displays outdoors, on house walls and even on outbuildings such as the garage or shed. They are mainly for summer displays since plants, even if hardy, often do not survive winters in these containers, except in areas where winters are very mild. Hanging baskets or wall containers are relatively small, and the soil in them can quickly freeze solid. There is not much one can do to prevent this, except to hang baskets of plants in a cool but frost-free greenhouse during freezing weather.

CHOOSING AND USING HANGING BASKETS

Traditionally hanging baskets are made from a widely spaced mesh of strong galvanized wire and are bowl-shaped. They are generally supported with three chains. Plants can be planted right through the wires in the sides to create a ball of colour. Such wire baskets are inclined to dry out rapidly in warm weather, so frequent watering is a must – at least twice a day.

Modern hanging baskets are generally made from moulded plastic and are again bowl shaped and supported with chains. Some include a built-in drip tray and others have a water reservoir to cut down on the frequency of watering. Being non-porous they do not dry out as rapidly as wire baskets.

One of the drawbacks of moulded-plastic baskets is that you cannot insert plants in the sides. So unless you plant some very long trailing plants, quite a lot of the basket is visible. And the bottom of a plastic basket is not one of the most pleasing sights!

No matter what type of basket you choose, select larger rather than smaller ones, because the smaller they are, the quicker they dry out. Small baskets also very much restrict planting designs. The largest baskets are at least 30cm (12in) in diameter and have a depth of 15–20cm (6–8in).

There are numerous places to hang baskets. House walls are the most obvious places, but they can also be hung in porches and used to decorate garages and sheds. Do not set them too high, or you may have problems with watering. It is also important to avoid windy spots; strong winds can do a lot of damage to baskets and plants.

Choose metal brackets to support hang-

ABOVE *Wall-mounted baskets make excellent containers for colourful summer bedding such as petunias, lobelia and impatiens, which have been planted through the sides of the container to hide it, as well as in the top.*

ABOVE RIGHT *Unlike hanging baskets, terracotta wall pots do not sway around in the wind but since they do not hold much soil they can dry out quickly. However, they have the advantage of being attractive, even when empty.*

RIGHT *With traditional wire hanging baskets you can create balls of colour with plants such as impatiens, lobelia and ivy-leaved pelagoniums, as they can be planted all round the container.*

ing baskets and make sure they are securely screwed to the wall or other support. Baskets are quite weighty, especially when they have just been watered.

WALL POTS

These pots look like flower pots or other containers that have been cut in half so that they can be mounted flat against walls. They can be used like hanging baskets, and an advantage over hanging baskets is that they do not sway around in the wind, so they can be used in more exposed areas.

The majority of wall pots are made from terracotta. Being made of clay, they are inclined to dry out rapidly in warm weather. They come in various shapes and sizes and are comparatively inexpensive.

Rather more expensive are lead wall pots in traditional styles. These are very much 'at home' on the walls of period houses.

There are also metal half baskets for mounting flat against walls – reminiscent of hay baskets for horses. These can be lined with black plastic sheeting before being filled with soil. You can make slits in the plastic and plant through the sides.

PLANTING BASKETS AND WALL POTS

Generally lightweight soils are best for baskets and wall pots, so all-peat potting soil is recommended.

WIRE BASKETS

When planting a wire basket first line the inside to hold in the soil. Traditionally wire baskets are lined with sphagnum moss, and aesthetically this is still the best. Alternatively you could use a synthetic medium for a liner; there are a number of different ones available. Use according to the manufacturer's instructions. Black plastic sheeting can also be used; punch some holes in the bottom for drainage.

Once the basket is lined it can be planted. To make this job easier for you, steady the basket by standing it on top of a large flower pot.

The arrangement of plants, especially summer bedding plants, generally has trailing kinds planted in the sides and around the edge, and upright, bushy kinds in the centre. To accomplish this, first place a shallow layer of soil in the bottom of the basket, lightly firm it, and then insert some trailing plants through the wires so that their roots rest on the soil surface. If you are using plastic or some other synthetic liner you will have to make slits in it so that you can push the roots through. Sphagnum moss can simply be parted with the fingers to make room for roots. Then add more soil and lightly firm it. Insert some more trailers, then position the busy plants in the centre. Fill in with more soil and finally plant trailers around the edge. Make sure you leave a space of 2.5cm (1in) between the soil surface and the top of the basket so that there is room for watering.

Wall baskets are planted the same way.

MOULDED-PLASTIC BASKETS

With moulded-plastic baskets simply add soil to about half the depth, lightly firm it, then position some bushy plants in the centre, followed by trailers around the edge. Fill in with more soil and lightly firm it. Do the same for wall pots.

After planting, gently water the plants thoroughly to settle them in, using a watering can fitted with a sprinkler.

ABOVE *Planting a traditional wire hanging basket. Line it with sphagnum moss, then partially fill with soil. Plant some trailing plants through the wires in the sides, add more soil and finish with a bushy plant in the centre and trailing plants around the edge. Planting in this way results in a ball of colour, once the plants have grown sufficiently.*

CHOOSING AND USING PLANTS

Plants chosen for hanging baskets and wall pots are usually temporary bedding plants that bloom for one particular season, generally summer. There are some permanent plants that can also be used, if desired. Bear in mind that in areas where the temperature drops below −4.5°C/25°F it can be difficult to winter any plants in baskets or wall pots outdoors because the soil quickly becomes frozen solid in freezing weather. If you wish to overwinter planted baskets and pots, keep them in a cool but frost-free greenhouse.

Most plants recommended here have already been described in Chapters 1 and 2, so check there for more detailed descriptions of them.

FOR SUMMER

Many people plant glorious mixtures of summer bedding plants in baskets and wall pots: trailing lobelia, sweet alyssum (*Alyssum maritimum*) with its masses of white flowers, and petunias, with perhaps zonal pelargoniums or bush fuchsias in the centre, maybe with silver-leaved cineraria. There is nothing wrong with such designs and indeed they look most attractive in an English cottage-style garden, but the trend is towards simpler designs using fewer plants, and even towards single-colour designs coordinated with the house colours.

As with window boxes watch the background. If it is cluttered, go for plants of one colour. If plain, then by all means use plants in mixed colours if you wish.

For shady locations use plants in light colours, such as pale yellows, cream, white, light pinks, and so forth, as they will show up much better than strongly coloured plants.

Popular basket plants for the shade are pendulous fuchsias and pendulous tuberous begonias (*Begonia* x *tuberhybrida,* Pendula group) plus the bedding impatiens or busy lizzie. With these you could have a bushy centrepiece of, say, silver-leaved cineraria, or perhaps a clump of green and white striped spider plant.

Summer-flowering pansies are highly recommended for baskets and will flower well in partial shade. They can be obtained in separate colours, so they are ideal for single-colour designs. Or try blue and white pansies with silver-leaved cineraria if you want a 'cool' design.

Plants that need sun include multiflora or small-flowered petunias, ivy-leaved pelargoniums, verbena hybrids and lobelia, all of trailing habit. For bushy growth try the bedding calceolarias (*Calceolaria integri-*

folia) with their masses of small yellow flowers. If you want a flower that spreads, there are gazanias, which revel in hot, dry conditions. A particularly pleasing design includes yellow calceolarias as a centre-piece, with yellow, grey-leaved gazanias around the edge.

Zonal pelargoniums make a good centre-piece for trailers like petunias and verbenas. Or plant a bushy heliotrope with pink or red ivy-leaved pelargoniums.

For something a bit more unusual try dwarf bushy nasturtiums (*Tropaeolum majus*); these are hardy annuals that have brightly coloured flowers in shades of red, orange, yellow, pink and white. Seeds of these can be sown directly in the baskets in mid spring. They do best in full sun.

Black-eyed Susan (*Thunbergia alata*) is an excellent half-hardy annual for hanging baskets or wall pots. The rounded yellow flowers have a dark 'eye', or centre, and are produced freely from early summer to early autumn. They do best in full sun.

FOR SPRING, AUTUMN AND WINTER

Pansies are now becoming very popular basket plants, especially those that bloom throughout winter in mild areas and well into spring. What is more, they tolerate partial shade. Try a combination of winter pansies and trailing ivies (the latter are permanent plants).

Other useful bedding plants for spring flowering are double-flowered daisies and polyanthus, or coloured primroses. Once again provide contrast in shape and colour by planting trailing ivies around the edge of the basket. Both of these plants are shade tolerant.

Permanent trailing plants for spring flowering are cultivars of periwinkle (*Vinca minor*) with starry blue, purple or white flowers, suitable for growing in shade or partial shade. Try growing miniature spring bulbs in the centre of the basket.

For winter colour try cultivars of *Erica carnea* (*E. herbacea*) in sunny positions.

ABOVE *A typical summer design for a hanging basket: bushy pelargoniums and French marigolds surrounded by impatiens or busy lizzie. Other plants for creating height include heliotrope (which is sweet-scented) and dwarf African marigolds (which are not!).*

The flowers of this heath come in shades of pink, red or white. No other plants are needed with them.

Another winter-flowering heath is *Erica* x *darleyensis*. This comes in similar colours, but an especially attractive cultivar is 'Silberschmelze' ('Molten Silver'), with its white flowers carried in very long spikes from late autumn until mid spring in mild areas.

Both of these heaths are lime-tolerant, though they grow better in lime-free soil. The heaths are permanent plants and can be kept in baskets for several years. To keep them compact trim off the old, dead flower heads in the spring before new growth commences.

Autumn is a time when hanging baskets can be colourless, but they need not be if you plant them with dwarf chrysanthemums, especially the suncharms and American cushion mums that are described on page 30.

CAMELLIAS IN BASKETS

An extremely unusual but nevertheless interesting and appealing idea has recently emerged from New Zealand – growing camellias in hanging baskets. At first this sounds impossible, because most camellias are eventually large, upright, bushy shrubs. However, small but flowering-size plants of somewhat trailing or pendulous habit can be planted (one per basket) and the young growths trained, by judicious tying, to grow outwards and downwards, over the edge. Obviously when a plant starts to outgrow a basket it can be taken out and planted in the garden. Camellias in baskets would also make pleasing features in a cool greenhouse or conservatory.

Good camellias for growing in baskets are the free-flowering cultivars of *C.* x *williamsii*. These bloom in the spring, producing flowers in shades of pink, red or white.

Camellias must be grown in lime-free soil, ideally an all-peat type, and they thrive in partial shade. Make sure the plants are

in a position that does not receive early morning sun, as this can damage frozen flower buds.

Do bear in mind that in areas subject to cold winters ($-12°C/10°F$ and below) it would be advisable to hang planted baskets in a cool but frost-free greenhouse during frosty or very cold weather, otherwise plants may be damaged or killed, especially if the soil ball remains frozen for a long period.

ABOVE *A hanging basket planted for winter. It combines a hebe, euonymus, pansies and trailing ivy. The soil must not be allowed to freeze solid for prolonged periods over winter.*

OPPOSITE *Ivy-leaved pelargoniums, with their trailing habit of growth and floriferous nature, are among the best plants for providing summer colour in hanging baskets.*

4

Balconies and Roof Gardens

Balconies and flat roofs can be made very colourful with a little thought and planning. Containers really come into their own in these situations.

CONTAINERS AND THE WEIGHT PROBLEM

It's not a good idea to put unnecessary weight on balconies and flat roofs, so lightweight containers are recommended, such as plastic or fibreglass tubs, troughs and so on. There is a wide choice of these on the market.

To keep them light, fill the containers with lightweight potting soil, such as an all-peat type. Growing bags are also extremely useful for growing plants on balconies and roof gardens (see Chapter 6). There is no reason why colourful bedding plants as well as vegetables can't be grown in them. Cascading and trailing plants will completely hide the bags which, after all, are primarily utility containers.

Provided the roof or balcony is strong enough, you could even consider having a mini-pool in a tub (see Chapter 5).

However, one must be particularly care-ful with flat roofs. Some of these will not take much weight at all and are not intended to be used as outdoor living spaces. This certainly applies to those flat roofs of house extensions that are simply boarded and covered with roofing felt. Even lightweight containers filled with all-peat soil can be surprisingly heavy immed-iately after watering and a collection of, say, a dozen or so could be too much for some roofs. It may be advisable to place containers around the edge of the roof, the area of greatest strength, rather than grouping them, say, in the middle, which is the weakest part.

Slightly raise the containers off the roof floor with blocks of wood to allow the free drainage of surplus water and to ensure good air circulation. This will benefit both the plants and the roof.

It would be advisable to consult with an architect or structural engineer to deter-mine to what extent a roof can be used for growing plants. You should also consult with your local planning authority to find out whether it is legal to garden on a roof in your area and to find out if there are any particular safety measures you should be taking.

OTHER CONTAINERS

Some containers, like hanging baskets and wall pots, of course, do not contribute to weight; they are great for balcony and rooftop gardening. If there are window-sills, then window boxes can be planted and installed (see Chapter 2). If a balcony has a wall around the edge it may be possible to mount window boxes on top of this. Each should have a drip tray underneath it, for obvious reasons, and even more importantly the boxes should be securely fixed to the wall by means of suitable metal brackets.

WIND AND SUN

Being high up, balconies and roofs are often more prone to the effects of cold winds than lower levels. Wind can lash plants around and damage them. Drying winds can quickly dry out the soil and give the foliage windburn. Plants may also receive too much sun. Extremely hot sun may not only damage the plants themselves, it can also dry the soil.

If you know that wind or sun is going to be a problem, try to choose plants that will tolerate them. Or provide some sort of protection against the elements.

Rather than trying to block out the wind entirely with solid panels that could look awkward or lead to turbulence as the wind travels over them, filter or slow down the wind with trellis panels. Ready-made wooden ones are generally available up to 1.8m (6ft) in height. When fixing them to the boundary walls or elsewhere make sure that they are really secure. One can only partially screen balconies, of course; perhaps trellis panels at each end would do the trick.

Trellis panels make ideal supports for climbing plants, and these would further help to provide wind protection. Choose really tough climbers for the screens and

grow them in tubs of suitable size. Ivies immediately come to mind, especially cultivars of *Hedera helix*, which is the toughest species. Climbing roses of modest stature are comparatively tough and so, too, is the winter-flowering jasmine, *Jasminum nudiflorum*, whose yellow flowers are particularly welcome in the dark days. The climbing hydrangea, *Hydrangea petiolaris*, is an adaptable plant, tolerating shade and atmospheric pollution, and producing large heads of greenish white flowers in early summer.

PLANTS THAT LIKE PLENTY OF SUN

With collections of both temporary bedding plants and permanent plants you can have colour and interest all year round. I will not discuss bedding plants in depth here since they have been covered in Chapter 1, and you will also find them mentioned again in Chapter 2 and Chapter 3. Suffice it to say here that if conditions are suitable, they can enhance any balcony or roof garden.

There are many permanent plants like

ABOVE *Balconies can be very colourful with lightweight containers of various kinds, plus hanging baskets. These have been planted with impatiens and nephrolepis fern, which acts as a cool foil, and both are suitable for shady conditions.*

shrubs that can be grown in tubs and that love hot, sunny conditions. Rock rose (*Cistus*) immediately springs to mind; it is a small, evergreen bushy plant that produces single rose-like blooms in pink or white during summer. Many of these have pleasantly aromatic foliage, and the fragrance is brought out by hot sun so that your balcony or roof garden could end up smelling like Mediterranean maquis. Rock rose is only suited to mild climates, and will tolerate minimum temperatures of −5°C (23°F).

The shrubby cinquefoils (*Potentillas*) also revel in the sun, and with their mainly yellow flowers make ideal companions for rock roses. They flower continuously all summer.

Lavenders can be grown with these for colour and texture contrast. They have greyish, aromatic evergreen foliage and blue flowers in summer.

Another grey-leaved evergreen shrub well worth growing with other plants, but only in mild climates, is *Senecio laxifolius*. The somewhat oval leaves are silvery-grey and covered with white felt on the under-

sides. Summer brings on bright yellow daisy flowers; some people dislike them and cut them off before they develop.

Some of the smaller olearias or daisy bushes are ideal for our purpose but are suited only to mild climates. The evergreen *O.* x *stellulata* has a rather sprawling habit and produces heads of white daisy flowers in late spring or early summer.

Escallonias are mild-climate evergreen shrubs, but where they can be grown they make a marvellous show of red, pink or white flowers in early summer. The smaller-growing hybrids and cultivars are suitable for tubs.

Dwarf conifers would be ideal for sunny balconies and roof gardens. Provided the atmosphere is not polluted, dwarf pines would thrive. Try *Pinus sylvestris* 'Beuvronensis', which is very hardy and makes a dome-shaped specimen. Equally hardy is the mountain pine (*Pinus mugo*) and its cultivars, which have very dense dark green foliage. All pines are evergreen.

There are many sun-loving alpines and dwarf perennials such as houseleeks (*Sempervivum*); sedums of all kinds; the red valerian (*Centranthus ruber*), with heads of small red, pink or white blooms over a long period in summer and autumn; and a veritable galaxy of small silver- or grey-leaved plants like *Anthemis cupaniana*, with white daisy flowers in summer; *Artemisia schmidtiana* 'Nana', which forms a neat mound of feathery silver-grey foliage; and for mild areas *Convolvulus cneorum*, with silky, silvery foliage and white, saucer-shaped flowers in summer and the curry plant (*Helichrysum angustifolium*) (it really does smell of curry), with narrow intensely silvery leaves and yellow flowers.

PLANTS THAT TOLERATE WIND

For windy sites certainly all of those small hardy evergreens mentioned in Chapter 1 can be recommended, but some larger shrubs may be required to give height:

BAMBOO (*Arundinaria japonica*) — Although only moderately hardy, this bamboo takes wind in its stride. The wind easily passes through its clump of olive green canes, rustling the long, lance-shaped, dark evergreen leaves.

SMOKE BUSH (*Cotinus coggygria*) — This very hardy shrub is noted for its autumn leaf colour, which comes in flame shades.

If you want colour in the summer as well, choose one of the purple-leaved cultivars.

SILVER BERRY (*Elaeagnus commutata*) — This extremely hardy shrub has intensely silver foliage and, in late spring, fragrant white flowers.

KERRIA JAPONICA 'VARIEGATA' — This shrub gives colour and interest in spring and throughout summer. The deciduous foliage is variegated creamy white, and yellow flowers are produced in the spring. A pleasing picture is created when spring-flowering bulbs are planted around it, such as blue grape hyacinths (muscari).

One might think that some of the tall ornamental grasses are highly unsuitable for windy situations, but in fact they are very wind resistant; wind filters easily through the stems so that they do not flatten. All of these grasses associate particularly well with shrubs, providing dramatic contrast in leaf shape, texture and colour.

ABOVE *Provided roofs are strong enough to take the weight, beautiful gardens can be created high above the city streets. Climbers and shrubs have been used to soften the walls to make a cool, well-screened area to sit in. Pelargoniums, impatiens and hydrangeas have been added for summer colour.*

RIGHT *Pots of petunias, lobelia, fuchsias and pelargoniums create an abundant, lush look on a roof garden.*

BELOW *Good use has been made of vertical space in this roof garden by growing climbers up the walls. The perimeter railings make a home for wisteria and other climbers.*

AMUR SILVER GRASS (*Miscanthus sacchari-florus*) – Often planted as a windbreak in gardens, this plant can grow up to 3m (10ft) in height. It has narrow, medium green leaves that arch over.

GARDENER'S GARTERS (*Phalaris arundin-acea* 'Picta') – One way to contain this grass is to grow it in a tub. In gardens it is inclined to spread vigorously. But it is one of the most beautiful of the ornamental grasses, with its white and green striped foliage that rustles in the wind. This is a lower-growing grass at only 60cm (2ft) in height; it is very hardy.

ZEBRA GRASS (*Miscanthus sinensis* 'Zeb-rinus') – This plant grows to about 1.2m (4ft) in height, somewhat lower than the species that can reach about 1.8m (6ft). The arching leaves of the cultivar are banded with yellow. It is a very hardy grass.

FEATHER GRASS, OR NEEDLEGRASS (*Stipa gigantea*) – This plant is not so hardy and therefore recommended only for areas where minimum temperatures are not below −12°C (10°F). It can grow to about 1.8m (6ft) in height. The virtually evergreen foliage is greyish green and in summer bold, attractive silvery purple plumes of flowers are produced.

Mini-Pools

Creating a mini-pool, complete with water lilies and other aquatic plants, in a large tub or similar container is easily accomplished and makes a pleasing feature on a sunny patio or even on a balcony or flat roof. Water adds new dimensions to a garden: there is movement when wind ruffles the surface of the water, and there are reflections when it is calm. Sun glinting on the water adds additional atmosphere.

WHAT CONTAINER?

A good size for a small pool is something around 90cm (3ft) in diameter, about the size of a wooden tub or half barrel. You may find other containers of suitable size, such as large circular concrete tubs. The pool should be at least 45cm (18in) deep, so avoid any very shallow containers.

Obviously these containers need to be waterproof, but this is easily accomplished by lining them with a butyl-rubber pool liner. Alternatively use one of the cheaper plastic pool liners. Incidentally black is a good colour for a liner – it creates a sense of depth in a pool.

The simplest arrangement is to stand the

water container right on pavement, pebbles or bare soil. If you are quite ambitious, you could cluster a group of mini-pools – perhaps three – together. This arrangement would create more impact than a single pool and, of course, give you more scope for growing plants.

You could also sink mini-pools to their rims in soil alongside a patio with their edges disguised by flat pieces of rock. This not only creates a more natural appearance but ensures the water temperature does not fluctuate wildly, as happens when tubs are above ground.

Suitable moisture-loving plants can then be planted in the surrounding soil which is generally kept moist by the pool overflowing periodically when it rains or when you replenish it with fresh water. Typical plants for the pool surrounds include astilbes, with plumes of feathery red, pink or white flowers in the summer; plantain lilies (hostas) with their bold foliage; and bog primulas, with candelabras of yellow, orange, pink or red flowers in summer.

It is best to choose small plants, or miniature versions of plants, for the surrounds so that they are in scale with the pool and do not swamp it visually.

OPPOSITE *A wooden tub or half barrel is easily turned into a mini-pool, complete with water lilies and other aquatic plants, creating an unusual feature for a sunny patio, balcony or roof garden. Do not place it underneath a tree as fallen leaves will rot and pollute the water.*

PLANTING THE CONTAINER

The planting period for aquatics is between mid- and late spring. Most people will prefer to plant water lilies and other aquatic plants in special plastic lattice aquatic baskets. Small baskets are adequate for the plants recommended here.

Heavy loam is the best soil to use for aquatics. Place some in the bottom of the basket, firm it well, then set a plant in the middle and fill in with more loam, again firming well. Finish off with a layer of pebbles to prevent the surface being washed away.

Then gently lower the baskets into the water. It is best not to lower newly planted water lilies to the full depth to start with. At first lower them so that only a little water covers their crowns. Then lower them gradually as they grow. This is most easily accomplished by standing the basket on bricks and then removing the bricks one at a time as the lilies get larger. Miniature

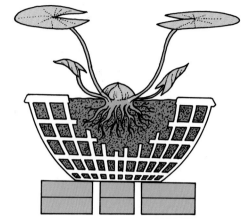

water lilies can be grown in water as shallow as 30cm (12in).

The other aquatics described in this chapter are marginal plants and only need a few centimetres (inches) of water over their roots. Grow them around the edge of the tub.

The alternative way to grow water lilies and other aquatics is directly in a tub with no basket. Plant them in a 10–15cm (4–6in) deep layer of heavy loam placed in the bottom of the water container. The loam can be mounded up the sides of the tub for the marginal plants.

LEFT *Water lilies and other aquatics can be planted in special plastic lattice aquatic baskets. The crown of each plant should be at soil level.*

LEFT *There are several miniature water lilies that are suitable for cultivation in a tub, as well as numerous small restrained marginal plants such as variegated sweet flag with its grassy foliage.*

Now to the arrangement of plants in a tub. One miniature water lily will be adequate for a 90cm (3ft) diameter pool. Place it in the centre so that it has space to spread its leaves.

Some submerged oxygenating plants or 'water weeds' such as water milfoil (*Myriophyllum* species) should also be planted in the centre of the pool because they help to keep the water clear. These usually come in small bunches, and a couple of bunches will be adequate for a tub. Then set the marginal plants around the edge of the tub. You will not need many of these – two or three should be adequate.

MINIATURE WATER LILIES

These are the most popular miniature water lilies.

NYMPHAEA X PYGMAEA CULTIVARS – The smallest of all is 'Alba', which has white flowers 2.5cm (1in) in diameter and small, deep green oval leaves. 'Helvola' produces small, bright yellow flowers, each with a conspicuous boss of orange stamens. The blooms show up beautifully against the dark olive green, purple and brown mottled leaves.

MILLPOND WATER LILY (*Nymphaea odorata minor*) – This water lily is a small plant with beautifully scented starry flower in pure white, no more than 8cm (3in) in diameter. These are carried on attractive reddish brown stems. The leaves are medium green above and deep red underneath.

PYGMY WATER LILY (*Nymphaea tetragona*) – This is a very tiny species with white flowers and golden stamens, about 5cm (2in) in diameter. The oval leaves, 8–10cm (3–4in) across, are blotched with brown when young, and the undersides are red.

ABOVE *Water lilies (some of which have fragrant blossoms) not only add colour to a mini-pool but help to shade the water, important if fish are to be introduced. All pools should also contain submerged aquatics which oxygenate the water and help to keep it clear.*

ABOVE LEFT *Mimulus or monkey flower is a bog plant which will happily grow in shallow water. The summer flowers may be orange, red or yellow.*

LEFT *The mini water lily* Nymphaea pygmaea *'Helvola' is popular for tiny pools, the yellow flowers showing up well against the dark leaves.*

MARGINAL AQUATICS

One must be extremely careful when choosing marginal aquatics for a tub because some are very vigorous and tall. The following small-growing kinds, of restrained habit, can be recommended with confidence for the mini-pool.

ACORUS GRAMINEUS 'VARIEGATUS' — A cultivar of the sweet flag, this plant has grassy foliage which is variegated cream and deep green. The flowers are insignificant. Unfortunately this is not one of the hardiest marginal aquatics; indeed, it is not completely frost hardy.

DOUBLE MARSH MARIGOLD (*Caltha palustris* 'Flore Pleno') — This is one of the favourite marginals. It is a dwarf, compact plant with

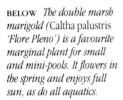

RIGHT *The bog bean's unusual hairy flowers make a good contrast to other aquatic blossoms.*

BELOW *The double marsh marigold (*Caltha palustris *'Flore Pleno') is a favourite marginal plant for small and mini-pools. It flowers in the spring and enjoys full sun, as do all aquatics.*

fully double, bright golden yellow flowers over a long period in spring and early summer. The bright green, shiny foliage makes an excellent background for the blooms.

BOG BEAN (*Menyanthes trifoliata*) — The bog bean thrives in shallow water and between early spring and early summer produces white flowers with fringed petals. The deep green leaves, composed of three leaflets, make an excellent background for the blooms.

WATER FORGET-ME-NOT (*Myosotis scorpioides*) — This aquatic variety is rather like the familiar bedding forget-me-nots, except that it thrives in shallow water. It differs from bedding forget-me-nots, too, in that it has smooth rather than hairy foliage. The rather loose flower heads consist of pale blue flowers that bloom for most of the summer. This is a popular and very easily grown marginal plant that will help to hide the edge of the pool.

DOUBLE-FLOWERED ARROWHEAD (*Sagittaria sagittifolia* 'Flore Pleno') — The distinctive foliage of this plant is arrow shaped, hence the popular name. In late summer double white flowers are produced.

Dwarf reedmace (*Typha minima*) – Normally one would avoid the reedmaces for tubs, as they are large, very vigorous aquatics, but not this species. It has grassy, deep green foliage and rounded dark brown seed heads that are the major attraction of the reedmaces. It is very easy to grow and really is suitable for tub culture.

CARE OF THE POOL AND PLANTS

The water in a newly created pool will quickly turn green with algae and become like pea soup. To many people this is, of course, devastating. But people familiar with pools will not worry about it, for they know that the water will gradually become clear of its own accord, provided the pool has been well planted with submerged oxygenating plants and other aquatics.

On no account change the water when it becomes green, otherwise the problem will never solve itself. The fresh water will simply become green again. Just leave the pool alone to settle down and remember that once the plants are established the water will gradually clear up. As water evaporates the pool should be replenished with fresh water. Apart from this a pool will need very little attention for a few years.

Every autumn as the plants die back for their winter rest, the dead foliage and stems should be cut back; if they are not, they will pollute the water as they decay, causing it to turn brown. Cut off dead material cleanly just above water level, not below it, as any hollow stems will become filled with water, and this can cause the crown of the plant to rot. If any leaves from deciduous trees find their way into the water during the autumn they, too, should be removed immediately.

Pygmy water lilies could be damaged by severe frosts, so if you feel they are at risk remove them to a tub in a frost-free but cool greenhouse for the winter; this is easily done if they are growing in aquatic baskets.

A small electric pool heater placed in the water during the winter will help to prevent the water freezing solid during severe weather.

It is not necessary to empty and clean out a pool each spring. A healthy-looking pool should be left undisturbed. However, marginal plants will need to be lifted, divided and replanted every two or three years in mid- to late spring as they start to become congested. The technique is the same as for border perennials – each clump should be split into a number of portions, discarding the old declining centre part and saving the young outer portions for replanting. Replant the divisions immediately – do not allow them to dry out.

Miniature water lilies can be left undisturbed for four or five years, when they may then need lifting and dividing in mid- or late spring. Discard the old central crown and retain the outer portions.

Submerged oxygenators may need surplus growth thinned out each spring to prevent congestion. Every two or three years lift them completely, divide and replant.

When a pool no longer seems as clean as it was, then that is the time to empty it completely, scrub it out and replant with freshly divided plants. Again the best time for a complete clean-out is mid- to late spring.

In summer dead flower heads should be removed from plants so that they don't fall into the water and foul it. Also, do not allow plants to set seeds since this only exhausts them. Plants should be fed each spring, unless they are being lifted and divided , by inserting a perforated sachet of aquatic plant fertilizer into the soil next to each plant. The fertilizer will slowly release nutrients during the growing season.

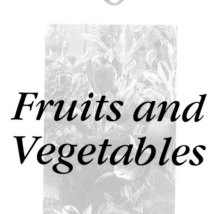

Fruits and Vegetables

Containers can give small gardens the extra space they need for growing fruits and vegetables. If edible plants are chosen carefully for their size, cultural needs and appearance, they can bring both decoration and harvest to the patio. Many fruit trees are quite ornamental, especially when in blossom and when they are bearing their fruits. And the more attractive-looking vegetables certainly do not seem out of place on a patio. Most herbs are compact, pretty plants that look quite at home in containers.

PATIO FRUITS

Many fruit trees can be grown in containers. Wherever possible choose dwarf trees. Varieties are budded or grafted by nurserymen on to special dwarfing rootstocks that keep the trees small and compact. Make sure you check which rootstocks the trees have been grafted on to when buying – ask for ones suitable for container growing.

APPLES AND PEARS – These most popular fruits are available on dwarfing rootstocks. Buy them as dwarf bush or dwarf pyramid trees. The former has a rounded, bushy shape and the latter is pyramid-shaped, as the term implies.

With apples and pears one needs to grow several cultivars together to ensure cross pollination and therefore good crops of fruits. The cultivars must all flower at the same time and they should be compatible – that is, capable of fertilizing each other. Garden centres and specialist fruit suppliers will advise on the best cultivars to grow together.

CHERRIES – Not so long ago cherries were not grown by many amateur gardeners because they grew into such large trees. Now, however, cherries are obtainable on dwarfing rootstocks and can be grown as dwarf bush or dwarf pyramid trees in containers. As you will probably need only one tree, buy a self-fertile cultivar that does not need to be cross pollinated.

PLUMS – At one time these, too, were only available as standard-sized trees, but like cherries they can now be grown as dwarf trees. A self-fertile cultivar on a dwarfing rootstock may be grown as a dwarf bush or dwarf pyramid tree.

PEACHES, NECTARINES – Both of these (a

OPPOSITE *The satisfaction of growing your own fruit and vegetables comes in being able to pick and eat them at exactly the right moment. Citrus fruits make very handsome tub plants and if you live in a frost-free climate they can be left outside all year round; otherwise give them glass protection over the winter. Some varieties of citrus have variegated foliage.*

ABOVE *Apples and pears on dwarfing roofstocks make ideal tub plants for a sunny patio. Several different cultivars are needed to ensure cross-pollination of the flowers. Pruning can be a skilled and time-consuming task.*

nectarine is simply a smooth-skinned form of the peach) will grow in containers, so long as you get dwarf bush trees. Only one tree of each need be grown, as cross-pollination is not required. However, bear in mind that peaches and nectarines flower early in the year before pollinating insects are around and therefore the flowers have to be pollinated by hand. This is quite easily accomplished with the aid of a soft artist's paintbrush. Gently dab the centre of each flower in turn with the brush so that you transfer pollen from one to another.

FIGS — These are very decorative trees, with their large leaves that create a rather exotic atmosphere. When grown naturally they make large specimens, but by restricting the roots in a container they can be kept as small bush trees. Unless they are being grown in a frost-free climate, figs should be removed into a frost-free yet cool greenhouse or conservatory over winter to prevent developing fruits from being damaged or killed by frost.

CITRUS FRUITS — The same routine applies to citrus fruits, which also make very handsome tub plants when they can be grown as dwarf pyramid or dwarf bush trees. If you live in a frost-free climate they can remain outside all year round; otherwise give them glass protection over winter. The most popular citrus fruits for tub culture are oranges, such as the sweet orange

(Citrus sinensis) and the Seville orange *(Citrus aurantium)*. These are also among the hardiest of the citrus fruits.

GRAPES – Dessert grapes grow remarkably well in containers and can be trained to various forms. Possibly the most convenient form for containers is the standard (trained to look like a tree), which consists of a single stem, at the top of which new growth is produced each year. It is this new growth that carries the fruit. In early winter every year all these shoots are pruned back to leave only one or two growth buds on each. (This is called spur pruning.) In cool, temperate climates dessert grapes are best grown in a cool greenhouse or conservatory all year round. But in warmer climates with frost-free winters they can remain outside throughout the year.

CONTAINERS AND PLANTING

Fruit trees look particularly attractive if they are grown in decorative containers. Whatever is used, a diameter and depth of 45–60cm (18–24in) is recommended. Square wooden planters make very attractive containers for fruits, especially if they are painted to match the house. Large terracotta pots in plain or ornate styles are also nice. Modern circular concrete tubs would be suitable for a contemporary setting.

However, young fruit trees should not be planted directly in large tubs, but rather started off in 30cm (12in) pots and gradually moved into larger containers. All containers should have a 2.5–5cm (1–2in) layer of pebbles in the bottom to ensure good drainage. This can be covered with a thin layer of rough peat or leafmould before adding the soil.

Planting and potting can be carried out in late autumn. Fruit trees are best grown in a potting soil containing loam, peat and sand. This is much heavier than, say, all-peat potting soil and therefore is better able to hold the trees securely. Also, there is less likelihood of the trees being blown over during windy weather. Work the soil thoroughly between the rootball and the side of the container and firm it well. Remember to leave a space of at least 2.5cm (1in) between the soil surface and the rim of the container to allow room for watering.

ABOVE *The Seville orange* (Citrus aurantium*) is one of the hardiest of the citrus fruits yet needs wintering in a cool greenhouse or conservatory in climates subject to hard frosts. It thrives in a large tub. Here it is being grown as bush trees.*

GENERAL CARE OF FRUIT TREES

For best results fruit trees need plenty of sun and shelter from winds. The soil should never be allowed to dry out, otherwise this will adversely affect development of the fruits.

Fruit trees respond to generous feeding, and throughout spring and summer they should be fed weekly with a liquid fertilizer containing a high proportion of potash, the element that plays a major role in fruit development and ripening.

If late frosts in the spring threaten to damage fruit blossoms, then cover the trees with fine-mesh plastic windbreak netting at night. If blooms are killed, fruits will not be produced.

Trees should not be allowed to carry excessively heavy crops, as this results in a much smaller crop the following year. If necessary, thin out the young fruits at an early stage of their development.

Fruit trees also need annual pruning, but this is quite a complex subject and varies according to the type of fruit and the form

PLANTING A STRAWBERRY BARREL

BELOW *Ready-made strawberry pots in various designs and materials are available and ideal for mini-patios. Every two or three years all plants need replacing with young ones, which are more fruitful.*

Strawberries take up a large amount of ground if planted in rows or beds in the traditional way. To economize on space and create a striking addition to the patio, balcony or roof garden, grow them in a strawberry barrel. The best time to plant strawberries is late summer, when they

will start cropping the following year.

A large wooden barrel will hold a lot of plants because they are planted in holes in the sides as well as in the top. Drill 5cm (2in) diameter holes in the side of the barrel, about 20cm (8in) apart each way and in a staggered pattern.

Make sure the barrel has some drainage holes in the base and then place a 2.5–5cm (1–2in) layer of pebbles in the bottom to help with drainage. Cover this with a thin layer of coarse peat or leafmould. Strawberries can be grown in all-peat potting soil or in a loam, peat and sand mix. Push the roots of the strawberry plants through the holes as the barrel is being filled with soil. Finish off with about three plants in the top.

Should you not wish to make your own container, you'll be happy to know that there are ready-made strawberry pots available. These are generally terracotta containers with holes in the sides. They are lovely when all planted up, but they do not hold as many plants as a large wooden barrel and they dry out quicker.

The soil for strawberries should be kept steadily moist and the plants fed regularly in spring and summer with a liquid fertilizer. In areas prone to frost make sure the flowers are protected, as frost can damage or kill them; cover the container at night with fine-mesh plastic windbreak netting.

in which the tree is grown. So for full details of pruning, and indeed other routine tasks such as fruit thinning, it is advisable to study a book on fruit growing. Regular spraying to control the numerous fruit pests and diseases may also be required, and again, such information will be found in a specialized book.

Each year in late autumn mature, established fruit trees should be repotted to replace the soil, which by then will be deteriorating in quality. This technique is described in Chapter 7.

PATIO VEGETABLES

Vegetables can be grown in conventional pots, tubs, barrels and troughs, which should be at least 30cm (12in) in diameter and depth, or better, 45–60cm (18–24in) wide and deep. They should be filled with an all-peat potting soil. But perhaps the most convenient way to grow vegetables on a patio, balcony or flat roof is to plant them in growing bags. These are purely utility containers consisting of a plastic bag about 1.2m (4ft) in length and 30cm (12in) wide, filled with potting soil, generally an all-peat type.

Growing bags are used only for one season, for instance, for a crop of tomatoes, or a succession of several shorter-term crops like radishes. Holes are cut in the tops of the bags for planting or sowing.

Most vegetables like plenty of sun, so choose a sunny part of the patio for them. This is especially important with tender kinds like tomatoes, sweet peppers and aubergines, all of which also need sheltered conditions.

Some of the taller vegetables will need staking, such as tall tomato cultivars and climbing French and runner beans. You cannot insert canes into growing-bags, so other methods of support have to be used. For instance, the bags could be positioned in front of a wall clad with trellis. The plants

can then be tied to this, or allowed to twine through it. You can buy growing-bag crop supports for tomatoes and similar plants in the form of a framework made from plastic-coated steel. These have 'feet' over which a growing bag is placed to anchor the framework. A similar support could easily be made at home by any handyperson.

WHAT TO GROW

TOMATOES – These are the obvious choice for patio growing bags and other containers. Choose cultivars intended for outdoor growing, either tall kinds, or dwarf bush tomatoes that do not need staking. Tomatoes are raised from seed indoors during early spring and planted out only when all danger of frost is over, in late spring or early summer. A growing bag will comfortably hold three tomato plants; four generally leads to overcrowding as the plants grow.

ABOVE *Growing bags are ideal containers for peas. This tall cultivar will crop heavily during summer from a spring sowing. The plants are well supported by means of proprietary growing-bag crop supports and wooden trellis panels.*

PEAS — You obviously cannot grow many peas in containers, so choose the most productive kinds, especially sugar, or edible-podded, peas. With these there is no wastage; the pods are gathered when young and cooked and eaten whole. Peas are hardy and can be sown in early or mid-spring, spacing the seeds about 5cm (2in) apart each way.

A novelty vegetable whose pods are also eaten whole is the asparagus pea (*Lotus edulis*). It has a low, rather sprawling habit and produces masses of very attractive deep red flowers that are followed by angular pods that should be picked when young and tender. Plants are frost tender. Sow directly in containers during late spring, spacing the seeds 20cm (8in) apart each way.

SWEET PEPPERS, AUBERGINES — Provided you live in an area with warm or hot summers capsicums, or sweet peppers, and aubergines, or eggplants, will crop well outdoors. There will not be much success with these in areas that have cool summers; there, plants are best grown under glass. Sweet peppers and aubergines are raised and grown in the same way as tomatoes.

BEANS — Among pod-bearing vegetables, climbing French beans grow well in containers. They produce heavier crops than dwarf beans so are more worthwhile. Being tender, they will not tolerate frost. Sow seeds directly in the containers between late spring and mid summer, spacing them 10–15cm (4–6in) apart.

Runner beans can also be recommended for growing bags, and other containers, and they are highly attractive when in flower. Some cultivars have scarlet flowers, while others are pink or white. Like French beans they are frost tender, but seeds can be sown in the containers outdoors during late spring or early summer. Space seeds 15cm (6in) apart.

ABOVE *French beans grow well in containers and crop during summer. Out of choice, grow climbing cultivars rather than dwarf beans (shown here) as they produce heavier crops.*

BELOW *Roundrooted cultivars of beetroot are ideal for salads. They are among the easiest root vegetables to grow and should be harvested while young and tender.*

RADISH — Small salad crops are, of course, ideal for containers. For instance, radishes can be sown in succession at two-week intervals throughout spring and summer. Sow thinly and keep well watered for rapid growth.

BEETROOT — Tiny beetroot, or beets, can be grown for salads, choosing early round-rooted cultivars and pulling them when young. Sow direct in containers during the spring and thin seedlings to 10cm (4in) apart each way.

LETTUCE – Choose some of the more ornamental kinds for the patio, such as non-hearting cultivars, with their deeply cut, frilly leaves (the leaves are picked individually as needed) and red lettuces. Aim for four or five plants per growing bag. Seeds can be sown direct during spring or raised in a greenhouse in pots and planted out when large enough.

CARROTS – Young early carrots are suitable for growing bags and other containers. Successional sowings can be made from early spring to late summer. Sow very thinly to avoid the necessity of thinning, which is a fiddly process, and pull them when young and tender.

WINTER CRESS (*Barbarea vulgaris*) – This salad green is good for salads and sandwiches and is easily grown in containers.

You can sow right in the bag or other container during early or mid spring, with additional sowings in summer. If you want a winter harvest, sow again in early autumn. Cover late sowings with cloches or some other form of frost protection. Thin seedlings to about 15cm (6in) apart and keep plants constantly moist.

COURGETTES – Courgettes, or zucchini, are very productive vegetables. They are essentially marrows, the fruits being picked when only 8–10cm (3–4in) in length. Choose bush cultivars rather than trailing kinds. Bear in mind that courgettes are frost tender. Sow direct during late spring, or raise plants in pots under heated glass, sowing in mid- to late spring and planting out when danger of frost is over. Two plants will be adequate for a growing bag, setting one at each end.

ABOVE *Courgettes or zucchini are very productive vegetables and therefore well worth growing on a patio. Choose bush cultivars rather than trailing kinds. A yellow-fruited cultivar is shown here.*

Fresh herbs on hand

Culinary herbs can be grown in ornamental terracotta pots or troughs and need a very well-drained soil and plenty of sun. Several small herbs could be planted in a large pot or trough. A group of containers planted with herbs could make quite an attractive feature on a patio. And the cook in the family will welcome the easy access to a range of useful kinds of herbs.

There is a very wide range of culinary herbs available but people find the following the most popular and the most useful.

Annuals

Several popular herbs are annuals and need to be sown afresh each year. Included here is parsley (*Petroselinum crispum*), which is sown direct in early or mid spring. Seeds are slow to germinate. Sometimes this

ABOVE *Mixed herbs look especially attractive in terracotta pots and make a pleasing as well as practical patio feature. They need plenty of sun.*

LEFT *Variegated and purple sages growing with marjoram – surely as pleasing as any flower display.*

RIGHT *Another use for a 'strawberry barrel' – a home for a collection of herbs. Avoid planting mint as it will quickly take over the barrel.*

plant will reseed itself. The tender basil (*Ocimum basilicum*) is sown outdoors during late spring, as is coriander (*Coriandrum sativum*) and dill (*Anethum graveolens*). Chervil (*Anthriscus cerefolium*) is a hardy biennial grown as an annual and can be sown from late winter to mid autumn in succession. Sweet marjoram (*Origanum majorana*) is a half-hardy annual sown during late spring.

PERENNIALS

Of the permanent perennial herbs suitable for growing in containers, common mint (*Mentha spicata*) must be the most popular. It is rampant, so it is best grown in a container on its own. Keep the soil moist. Mint can be grown in shade if desired. Lift and divide every two years in early spring. Sage (*Salvia officinalis*) is a popular perennial, as is thyme (*Thymus vulgaris*). Chives

ABOVE *Window boxes also make excellent containers for herbs. Pick off leaves or young shoots as needed.*

(*Allium schoenoprasum*) form neat clumps of foliage that have an oniony flavour. Lovely lilac-coloured flowers appear in late spring. Plants should be lifted and divided every two years in early spring. Pot marjoram (*Origanum onites*) is another useful culinary herb, as is wild marjoram or oregano (*Origanum vulgare*).

A tall herb for the back of a group is fennel (*Foeniculum vulgare*), which has beautiful feathery foliage. It bears yellow flowers in summer and would not look out of place in a group of ornamental plants.

Two very popular herbs are tall shrubs and should have containers to themselves. One is the sweet bay (*Laurus nobilis*), with large, evergreen, lance-shaped leaves that are aromatic. It responds well to regular clipping so it can be grown as a trained specimen, such as a pyramid or mopheaded standard. It is on the tender side, so in areas with hard winters it is best wintered in a frost-free but cool greenhouse.

The evergreen rosemary (*Rosmarinus officinalis*) has small, aromatic leaves and in spring produces tubular, lipped, mauve flowers. This is another rather tender shrub and needs winter protection under glass in cold areas. It is very decorative and could be included in a group of ornamental shrubs if desired.

Do not subject herbs to hard freezing. Winter in a cool greenhouse if necessary.

Year-Round Care

It cannot be denied that growing plants in containers is quite labour intensive, particularly during warm weather when they will need a lot of watering. Then there is feeding of plants (needed more often than plants growing in the garden), changing potting soil, moving plants into larger containers, the pruning of some permanent plants (although the same plants in the garden would also require this) and protection during the winter if you live in an area subject to severe frosts.

WATERING CONTAINER PLANTS

This will be a regular task in warm weather, when some containers may need checking twice a day. Do not neglect to check them regularly in cooler weather, too, even in winter, when the soil can still dry out, albeit more slowly.

Try not to let the soil become very dry,

nor water so much that it remains saturated. The way to test potting soil for moisture is to insert your fingers just below the soil surface. If the soil feels dry there, then water. Alternatively probe the soil with a soil-moisture meter.

Each time you water, water until it starts running out of the bottom of the container. This is the sign that the entire volume of potting soil has been moistened. To make sure that the spray of water is not too strong, forcing soil out of the container or damaging leaves, either use a watering can or a hosepipe fitted with a trigger-operated watering lance or nozzle.

If you are growing lime-hating plants such as rhododendrons, remember that some tap water may contain lime. The plants will object to this and their leaves will turn yellow. Instead collect and use rainwater.

To ensure your plants receive enough water while you are away, consider a temporary automatic watering system — say a drip system consisting of a main hosepipe fitted with thin tubes that continuously drip water slowly into the containers. This system can be run from a water reservoir (such as a small tank raised above the ground) or from the main water supply via a header tank with a control valve.

OPPOSITE *It is essential to winter plants prone to frost damage in a cool greenhouse or conservatory, which also makes a pleasant place to sit on sunny winter days.*

ABOVE *Watering is a regular task in warm weather when some containers may need checking twice a day. Water in the evening or early in the morning, and give enough water so that it starts to trickle out of the bottom of the container.*

SUPPLYING PLANT FOODS

Container-grown plants need more feeding than plants in the garden, for nutrients are washed out of the potting soil during watering. However, only feed plants while they are growing – in the spring and summer, never in autumn and winter. And do not apply extra fertilizer until plants are well established because new potting soil contains fertilizer, and this should be used up first before you start feeding.

Use a flower-garden or general-purpose fertilizer containing the main plant foods: nitrogen, phosphorous and potash. A fertilizer that is fairly high in potash is useful for flowering and fruiting plants since it assists in the production of blooms and fruits. Liquid fertilizers are the most convenient means of feeding container plants.

Summer bedding plants need feeding once a week or every two weeks, say from about six weeks after planting. Permanent plants can be fed every other week or weekly for fruits and for plants that are outgrowing their containers.

POTTING AND REPOTTING

Permanent plants like shrubs and trees should not be planted immediately in large containers (unless, that is, you purchase large specimens). Ordinary, small young specimens are better started off in smaller pots and gradually potted into larger sizes (two sizes larger each time) before the pots become packed with roots, until they are large enough for their permanent pots. Moving plants into larger pots like this prevents roots of young plants rotting from large volumes of wet soil around them.

Plants can be potted in early spring just before they come out of dormancy and start into growth again. The technique is as follows: first make sure that the plant's root-ball is moist. Ensure the container has drainage holes in the base, then spread a layer of pebbles over the bottom for good drainage. Cover this with a thin layer of rough peat or partially rotted leaves. Then put a layer of potting soil over the drainage layer and firm it in place. If you are planting just one plant put it in the centre of the container. (If you are planting several smaller plants, see the alternative method, below.) Adjust the depth of the soil layer if necessary, bear-

ing in mind that when potting is completed there must be a 12–25mm (½–1in) watering space at the top of the pot and that the top of the plant's rootball should be covered with 12mm (½in) of new soil.

Next fill the space between the rootball and the sides of the container with new potting soil, firming it with your fingers as you proceed, only lightly if all-peat, or moderately if it contains loam, peat and sand.

This technique should vary slightly if several plants are to be planted in a container such as bedding plants or small permanent kinds like shrubs or perennials. Prepare the container as described above. Fill it with potting soil and then make individual planting holes. Insert a plant in each and then firm the soil around them.

With either technique, water the plants gently but well to settle them in after planting, using a watering can fitted with a sprinkler.

REPOTTING

Repotting is a technique used for single permanent plants in containers like trees and shrubs, including fruit trees. It is a means of changing the potting soil without providing a larger container and it applies only to plants in their final, permanent containers. Potting soil has to be changed every so often because it starts to deteriorate in quality and then plants do not grow so well. Drainage and aeration may become poor and plant foods may have been leached out. In these conditions plants make poor or little growth.

How often should one repot permanent plants? Ideally fruit trees, which expend a lot of energy on fruit production, should be repotted each year in late autumn. You need not go to all this trouble with other trees or shrubs quite so often; once every two years should be sufficient. When they are dormant in late autumn is a suitable time for repotting deciduous trees or

shrubs, but evergreens are better repotted in mid spring.

Repotting often involves large containers, so two people may be needed for the operation. Place the container on its side. One person should then firmly tap the rim of the container with a block of wood while the other person gently pulls on the plant. The rootball should then slide out of the container. However, if the rootball sticks, work a long, sharp blade of some kind all around, between the rootball and the side of the container. Then try again to slide out the rootball.

Once the rootball is exposed it should be made smaller by about 5cm (2in) all around to allow space for fresh potting soil. Using a small handfork, tease away some of the old soil all around, including top and bottom. If necessary, some of the roots can be trimmed back by about 5cm (2in) with hand pruners.

ABOVE *It is best to pot plants just before the present pot becomes packed with roots. Prepare a pot about two sizes larger, putting pebbles in the bottom for drainage. Position the plant centrally on a layer of fresh potting soil, then work more soil well down between rootball and sides of pot.*

FAR LEFT *When planting several plants together, first fill the container with soil, then make a hole for each one. The design should be well thought out before you plant.*

containers, such as dwarf shrubs and perennials, heathers and dwarf conifers are usually left alone until the containers start to get overcrowded. Then the plants can be lifted and planted in the garden. The containers are cleaned, supplied with fresh soil and planted with new, young plants. Bear in mind that some plants can be divided into smaller portions, especially many perennials, so you may not need to replace all the plants with new ones that you removed. The best time for dividing perennials, and indeed for replanting containers, is in early spring.

Cover the plant's rootball with wet burlap to prevent it drying out while you wash out the container and dry it completely. Then put the plant back in its container and follow the step-by-step instructions on potting, earlier.

TOPDRESSING

In the years between repotting topdress your plants. This involves scraping away about 2.5cm (1in) or more of the old soil from the top of the container and replacing it with fresh potting soil. This is easily and quickly achieved and well worthwhile. Spring is the best time for topdressing.

OTHER SOIL CHANGES

The soil in containers used for temporary bedding plants should be changed every alternate year before it starts to deteriorate too much in quality. Simply remove all the old potting soil (this can be spread on the garden) and drainage material, thoroughly wash the inside to remove all traces of soil, allow it to dry completely, then replace the drainage layer and fill with new potting soil. The soil in hanging baskets and wall pots can be replaced each year in the spring before you plant them.

Groups of small permanent plants in

PRUNING PERMANENT PLANTS

The majority of permanent ornamental plants like shrubs and climbers do not need any pruning apart from the removal of dead and dying wood. However, there are some that need regular attention, as detailed below.

HEATHS AND HEATHERS, SANTOLINA (COTTON LAVENDER), SENECIOS AND LAVENDERS — These small shrubs need to have their dead flowers removed. This is quite a simple and quick operation. Trim off the dead flowers immediately after blooms have faded with a pair of sharp garden shears, but do not cut into the wood.

HYDRANGEAS — Leave on the dead blooms of hydrangeas until the spring in areas subject to frosts, as they help to protect the dormant buds just below.

Carefully cut them off with hand pruners taking care to avoid damaging the new buds.

RHODODENDRONS — Remove the seed heads as soon as flowering is over. It is not a good idea to allow these to develop, since most people do not save the seed and allowing them to fully develop uses up a lot of the plant's energy which would be better diverted to the production of flower buds for the following year's display. Rhododendron seed heads are easily removed by twisting them off, but take care to avoid damaging the new buds just below them as you do so.

FORSYTHIA — This shrub needs regular pruning immediately after flowering. Cut the old flowered stems back to young shoots lower down and remove some of the oldest wood, while retaining plenty of new or comparatively new growth.

KERRIA JAPONICA — This plant and its cultivars are pruned after flowering by cutting back old flowered stems to strong, young shoots lower down. Some thinning out of old shoots may also be required to encourage new growth from ground level.

ROSES (*Rosa*) — Some roses need annual pruning in early spring. Floribundas are pruned first by cutting out all weak and dead growth and then reducing the remaining strong stems to within 20cm (8in) of soil level. Make the cuts just above buds that face outwards. The bushes should have an open centre, free from any growth.

With climbing roses you should allow a permanent framework of stems to build up.

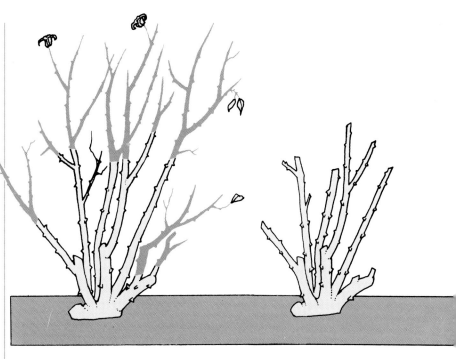

ABOVE *Floribunda roses need annual pruning in early spring, to encourage plenty of young, vigorous flower-producing growth.*

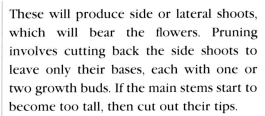

BELOW *A number of plants need to have their dead flowers removed to prevent energy-consuming seed production. Examples are rhododendrons (shown here), roses, heathers and bedding plants.*

These will produce side or lateral shoots, which will bear the flowers. Pruning involves cutting back the side shoots to leave only their bases, each with one or two growth buds. If the main stems start to become too tall, then cut out their tips.

Miniature roses do not need regular pruning. Simply remove any dead and dying wood as soon as you notice it.

SWEET BAY (*Laurus nobilis*), HOLLY (*Ilex*) AND BOX (*Buxus sempervirens*) — If these plants are grown as clipped specimens they should be trimmed as necessary during the summer to keep them neat.

Box can be trimmed with a pair of sharp garden shears, but the large-leaved sweet bay and hollies are better trimmed with hand pruners to avoid cutting the leaves in half. Cut leaf edges turn brown, creating an unsightly appearance. It can be rather slow and tedious cutting each shoot with hand pruners, but it is well worth the trouble in the long run.

WINTER JASMINE (*Jasminum nudiflorum*) — This climber should have some of its oldest and weakest wood cut out completely.

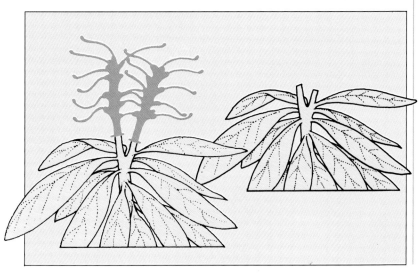

Then prune back old flowered shoots to leave only about 8cm (3in) of their base. Prune winter jasmine immediately after flowering.

SUMMER JASMINE (*Jasminum officinale*) – This is also pruned immediately after flowering. The oldest shoots should be thinned out to prevent congested growth, but do not reduce in length any of the remainder.

CLEMATIS – The large-flowered hybrid clematis need pruning, but the method varies according to type. The hybrids that flower from late spring to mid summer on wood formed the previous year, like 'Lasurstern' and 'Nelly Moser', can be left until growth starts to become congested. Then in late winter they can be cut down to within about 90cm (3ft) of soil level. In the spring they will make plenty of new growth.

Those clematis that flower during summer and autumn on the current year's shoots, such as 'Jackmanii Superba', should have all their growth cut back to just above soil level in late winter each year. Make the cuts right above strong growth buds. This sounds drastic, but they will make plenty of strong new growth in the spring.

PRUNING HERBACEOUS PERENNIALS

So far I have been discussing the pruning of woody plants such as shrubs and climbers. But herbaceous perennials also need annual attention. In the autumn the top growth dies down and the plants take a rest over winter. The dead growth should be cut down to soil level in the autumn. Evergreen perennials do not die back, but some of the leaves die and these should be removed as necessary.

The foliage of spring-flowering bulbs dies down each year in the summer, at which stage it can be cut off at ground level. On no account cut off bulb foliage before it has completely died down, other-wise you will jeopardize flowering the following year. The plants need this foliage to allow the bulbs to build up and gain strength for flowering again. Without foliage this will not happen and blooms will not be produced. In fact, to help in this building-up process, feed the bulbs with a liquid fertilizer two or three times in the spring after flowering while the foliage is still green.

TRIMMING BEDDING PLANTS

You should regularly remove the dead flower heads of bedding plants, as this encourages more to be produced and therefore extends the flowering period. This is perhaps more important with summer bedding plants, but spring-flowering kinds like polyanthus should be dead-headed, too. Seed production stops plants from producing more blooms, so if you prevent this from happening then the plants will quickly develop more flowers with the view to setting a crop of seeds. Admittedly it can be a tedious job going over the plants with a pair of flower scissors, but it is well worthwhile for the extended display.

LEFT *In hot areas some plants in containers, such as lilies, will suffer if the soil heats up too much. The containers may need to be shaded with sun-loving plants but the tops of the plants still enjoy plenty of sun.*

PROTECTING PLANTS FROM TEMPERATURE EXTREMES

A problem with container growing in areas that experience severe frosts in winter is that the potting soil can freeze solid for prolonged periods. The frost itself will not harm very hardy or tough plants; the problem is rather that it prevents them from absorbing water and therefore the plants could die of drought! One way to prevent this happening is to move the containers into a frost-free yet cool greenhouse or conservatory during severe weather. This will certainly be necessary for less-hardy and tender plants that could be damaged or killed by severe frosts.

Tough plants that can be left outside during severe spells could have their containers insulated to help prevent the soil from freezing solid. There are various natural materials one could use, like bracken or straw. The containers should be wrapped with a thick layer of these materials, which can be held in place with wire netting.

Although not aesthetically pleasing, thick wads of newspaper make excellent insulation and can be held in place in the same way. Fibreglass roofing insulation is another material that could be used.

Another possibility is plunging containers to their rims in the soil in a spare part of the garden. To prevent the ground around them from freezing, mulch with a 15cm (6in) deep layer of bulky organic matter such as peat, leafmould, chipped or pulverized bark, straw or bracken.

In hot areas it is not frost that is troublesome, it is the sun. Some plants like clematis, camellias and rhododendrons, and many shade-loving plants, suffer if the soil heats up too much. To help keep temperatures down in containers, shade them as much as possible with growth from other plants. Bushy plants grouped around containers will help to shade them, as will trailing plants cascading over the edge. Or place containers with heat-sensitive plants in more shady conditions where they will not receive the intense midday heat.

Index